"MOMMIE, WHAT IS A NIGGER?"
THE CASE OF THE CENTURIES

THOMAS JEFFERSON JACKSON
1869 - 1943

"MOMMIE, WHAT IS A NIGGER?"

THE CASE OF THE CENTURIES

MIA ISAAC
with six chapters of Public Domain information

IGIA
Innate Genius Intelligence Ability
Columbia, South Carolina

The author would like to thank Faye Chestnut, (editor), and Sandra Lemons (typist), for their assistance and support in researching this book. I could not have written without them.

Innate Genius Intelligence Ability, Co.
Post Office Box 3688, Columbia, South Carolina 29203
U.S.A.

Published in 1996 by Innate Genius Intelligence Ability, Co.
Copyright © 1996 by Mia Isaac
all rights reserved.

Chapters I, II, IV, V, VI, and VII previously written and in public domain

Distributed in the United States by IGIA
Printed in the United States of America

  Grateful acknowledgement is made to my grandfather, Thomas "Jeffie" Jackson, and my Grandmother, Queen Livingston Jackson, for keeping the "old book" which turned out to be the research for this book; Aunt Maryann Jackson Pough and my mother, Bessie Jackson Isaac, for giving the "old trunk with his old books to Pete because she likes to read just like Papa;" and for Aunt Janie Jackson Amaker for saving and giving to me "Papa's obituary."
  The contemporary photograph of my maternal Grandfather is from the Jackson family collection.

Library of Congress Catalog Card Number: 95-80261
ISBN: 0-9630229-2-X

(sic) - Yes, there are errors, but this is the way it was written in the original

DEDICATED TO

The Almighty God

The Family

and to
All Human Beings on this Earth of the human family especially African-American males and females.

"My people suffer from the lack of knowledge"
Bible

CONTENTS

Opening Statement vii

Chapter

I. The Formation of the Negro and other Beasts-then Man on the Sixth Day. 1

II. Biblical and Scientific Facts Demonstrating that the Negro is not an Offspring of the Adamic Family. . . .46

IV. Convincing Biblical and Scientific Evidence that the Negro is not of the Human Family 84

V. Cain's Offspring Soulless, as they were of Amalgamated Flesh 128

VI. Red, Yellow and Brown Skin Denoted Amalgamation of the Human Family with the Beast, the Negro 161

VII. That the Beast is Biped Animal, and not a Quadruped, is Proven by the Bible 201

Closing Statement 239

       The four years Game Plan (1996-1999). We had nine years (1990-1999)

Suggested Readings
Glossary
Dictionaries

OPENING STATEMENTS

An African American: My Heritage ©
February 27, 1995

By: Daniel Leon Isaac Jamison

OPENING STATEMENTS:

An African American: My Heritage ©

African-American means that my parents and I are descendants of Africans. *Heritage* means that some of the good, positive actions and teachings about Africa have been passed down to me from generation to generation.
The information that I will be sharing with you in this essay is researched information that my parents have read and talked about with me.
I asked my mother one night, "Mommie, what is a nigger?" She took out the old book that she had found in my maternal great grandfather's trunk, and we read some of what a writer had written about "What a negro is." We discussed the words negro, negress, negroid, nigger, colored, black, and African-American (see research). I learned from discussions with my parents that the words *negro, negroid* (males), *negress* (female), *nigger, colored*, and *black* are words that were applied to Africans and African-Americans by Europeans and European-Americans (caucasians). These names were applied

before the 1600's. The purpose of these negative names was to strip my ancestors of a belief in the Almighty God (their Creator), destroy the family arrangement, as well as all of their African heritage, culture, and contributions never allowing for them to serve in any political position(s); and force them to be slaves. Making my ancestors slaves meant that they would not be able to pass on to their children anything positive about Africa, God, the family, and the political system(s) that make laws to benefit all. The children would suffer down to this year, 1995.

The Africans and the African-Americans were not supposed to be able to use innate genius, innate intelligence, or their innate abilities in their own way. If European Americans learned that Africans or African-Americans did have "genius," they would take the person and the inventions that slaves had created as their own- Why? (Read the research)

My parents are helping me to learn that millions upon millions of our ancestors invented things, had excellent ideas, owned businesses, educated themselves, believed in the family, married, had strong family values, and trusted and believed in the Almighty God.

My maternal grandfather, paternal grandfather, and my daddy are car mechanics (My dad graduated from South Carolina State University receiving a business degree). No one taught them how to fix cars. All three of them will tell you "God gave me these skills."

I am not any of the negative names that my parents have discussed with me and which I have just shared with you. Neither is any other African American or anyone of African descent. I am an American because I was born in the country of America, but my ancestors were Africans, created by the Almighty God.

I must get an "education equal to my genius". I am proud of being an African American. Some day I will get married, have a family, and pass on this information to my children as my parents are teaching me.

Will you teach your children the truth about slavery and what a *nigger* is or is not? So that as we meet and associate with each other now, and in the 21st century, we will respect each other's heritage, work with each other, love one another, and love the God that has given all of us life.

Thank you.

       Daniel Leon Isaac Jamison

"Mommie, What is a Nigger?"
The Case of The Centuries ©

Plaintiffs	The plaintiffs are the people who wrote this book or the people who hold the opinions expressed therein.
vs.	
Defendants	The defendants are the people about whom this book is written or the people who refute the opinions expressed.

Have you ever been called a "nigger" by a person of the Anglo-Saxon ethnic group? How did you really feel? What do you think they meant when they called you "nigger"? If you are of African descent, have you ever called another person of African descent "nigger"? How do you think that person felt? What did you mean when you called the person "nigger"? How did you feel being called a "nigger" by another African American? What meaning did you apply to the word? What meaning is the Anglo-Saxon person applying to the word? Where did the word originate? How much weight does this word carry for some who are using it in 1995?

The case (research) that you will be reading about was found in an old trunk that belonged to my maternal grandfather, Thomas Jefferson Jackson. My grandfather was born on February 4, 1869, in Woodford, South Carolina. He died on December 24, 1943. I wish that I could tell you who my great-grandparents were on his side, but I cannot. My research has led me to know why, but I want to wait for one more fact to confirm my findings before I divulge the reasons.

Grandpa Jackson was a reader. He read the Bible, the newspaper (subscribed to the State newspaper), and different books. This case that I present is a case that I believe he read many times. I say this because of the way he kept records of important events in his life, the way he raised his ten children and five nieces and nephews. Therefore, he had in his house at one time, fifteen children. Grandpa Jackson was a loving person.

Grandpa believed in the family, and the

marriage arrangement. Why? His first and second marriages were recorded in his Bible by him. All of his children's birthdates were recorded in his Bible by him. Grandpa was a good, respectable husband, father, provider and protector of his wife and children. He was an honest man. People still talk about Jeffie Jackson and his family. He showed the same respect and care for others, also. Grandpa Jackson was a "gentleman." God created him as matter, mind, and soul. He was a moral person, and he taught and raised his children to be the same way.

Actually, my mother and my aunt Mammie found the old books, magazines and the State newspaper ordering blank in "papa's old trunk" as they were summer cleaning. My mother would always visit her sisters and brothers in South Carolina for the summers. So in the summer of 1978 when I visited Bluefield, West Virginia, with my friend; my mother went home to South Carolina. But I would meet her later, and we would both return home to New York together.

The two of them, my aunt and my mother, had decided to throw "papa's old trunk" away because it was deteriorating, but they took a last look into the trunk. They decided then not to throw away the "old trunk" or the things that were in it. Instead, they told me later, they decided that they would "save it for Pete (my mother said I was born so little that my Uncle Benjamin nicknamed me Pete) to look at; she loves to read things. She is just like Papa, reading something almost all of the time." When they gave it to me, I looked at everything and decided to keep the "old trunk" and all. I am still trying to figure out if my title for this manuscript shouldn't be *If the Old Trunk Could Talk*, or *Grandfather's Old Trunk*.

Over the years I would thumb through the Case (research) and read portions, picking up bits and pieces of what the writer was saying. But it was not until the summer of 1983 that I really planned, sat down, took my time after praying, and read the Case (research) all the way through. It took me two days. I took notes in a notebook as certain things were being revealed to me. What I learned from this Case (research) has shocked me to the point of my trying to literally destroy the book. I remember throwing the book up against the walls, taking it outside and stomping it, kicking it, crying and saying, "unh-unh, unh-unh." This is what some have been using for years, decades, centuries. This is what my grandfather had read, and in his own way because of this, he treated his children on the farm differently from how others might have treated their children. He did not use his children; they never wanted for anything. He planted enough to feed them, and to give to others. The family did not just work to make a living and have the White man to live off them also. They enjoyed their lives. All of his children went to school and got a good education in spite of the unjust laws that they were living under. He paid his taxes and respected the government (federal, state and local). All of his grandchildren know this about him, because other people still talk about Jeffie Jackson and his children/family.

Unjust laws, which have been born out of taught hate, stripping a people of their dignity on the level of the Almighty God, family, and protection by and from the federal, state, city and local government, have always been a great problem in America.

Rioting, killing, and destruction are not

what this research is about. In fact, I hope that I will never live to see or hear that anyone (especially African Americans) will carry out the above actions no matter what the verdict, sentence or action(s) by those in authority. African Americans must act with the dignity of those who struggled before them.

Dr. Martin L. King, Jr., along with many of African Americans, openly discussed and marched against injustices, and organized a bus boycott in December, 1955, in Montgomery, Alabama. This boycott lasted for over a year because the laws said that a White man should sit down before an African American woman who had worked hard all day. I still wonder how he got African-Americans to participate in this boycott in the month when Christmas was right around the corner. But, it was not Dr. King and the others; it was the time table of the Almighty God clocking in and spiritually engulfing all who would heed the call to eradicate injustice toward all human beings.

Now we are met with the call of the *"nigger"*. Let's put all of the findings pertaining to the *"nigger"* on the table. Research everything and everyone if you may. Let's bring it out and end it before the year 2000. I want you to take your time and go into the public library once or twice a week, taking your entire family, and read the *Negro Almanac*, a reference work on the African-American. Stop worrying about "I have to fix or eat dinner," or "My special program is on this evening." Just do it. Choose the day(s) and time. Call this time your sandwich dinner days. So, fix your sandwiches and beverage the night before, or the day you want to go. Take the car or walk to your nearest library. Eat your sandwich - dinner (food and drink) before you go inside; then go inside and find or ask the librarian for the book mentioned above or any other books that will interest you. Let the children do their homework, or if they may have already done such, you check the homework, sign it, and then start your research. Yes, this is going to be hard in the beginning, but keep at it. I guarantee you and the children will begin to warm up to reading/researching. Always discuss what you read. Ask other parents, also, to come with you. Let's feed our bodies, but to get African Americans out of the entrapment that you will read about from this case (research); you must also feed your brains, so that African Americans can restructure and empower their minds, hearts and actions back to the (1) Almighty God (clean morals, values), (2) family (marrying, two parents - raising our sons/daughters to become moral husbands/fathers and moral wives/mothers), (3) working (establishing their own business or, hiring out their skill to someone else's business), and (4) the governments (people who are serving in positions of the federal, state, city, and county government) . All of this with the help of the Almighty God's spirit before the year 2000.

I have always loved to read, write, pray, read my Bible, do research, and travel. I believe this hunger/desire to know for sure drove me to major in social studies/history. I have always had a desire to know. I react strongly to anyone who tries to tell me what I can not do; and never say to me when I am doing or discussing a positive idea, etc. "Those White people are not going to let you do that." I will always respond to those reactions. Most of the positive ideas that I think and talk about are to benefit all human beings - including White people, but particularly for African-Americans. So, since the idea is to help African-Americans, the people that will really not let me "do that" will be some African Ameicans. Some African American will not allow themselves to be taught by each other, sharing and giving certain restructuring and empowering information or products that will change their hearts, minds and actions. Some White people will simply structure the laws coming from the federal, state, city, local government and the school system to alter any positive ideas or programs that will help all of us. They will get these unjust laws passed because they have already elected those that will pass these laws. If you question the action behind the law, they will simply say to you "The law said ....," as though the law has life in it. A good example of this were/are the unjust laws that were written and passed in the United States Constitution which each state patterned their laws after to force African Americans into slavery mentally, physically, psychologically, financially and spiritually. It is similar to what you are told sometimes when an error has been made on a bill, "Oh, the computer made the error and we are sorry." The computer does not have life. It can only act because someone has programmed it and pushed the button. So who really made the error? Was it the computer or the person? Is it the law that causes people (especially African Americans) not to have strong, moral families, productive jobs, decent housing, and a quality education? Or, is it something that is innate in those who write these laws, pass these laws, and finally make sure that someone is there to enforce these laws.

My questions are always there, but actions and questions by others awakened that burning drive which I asked the Almighty God in prayer over forty years ago, and I continued throughout elementary school, junior high school, high school, college and as we attended the World's University. (Have you ever attended or visited the World's University? You are not an educated person until you have attended or visited the World's University without any inhibitions.)

Our research has proven to us that we should always use the word African-American when addressing- Blacks, and respect the use of names that anyone wants to be called. African

Americans must trace their heritage back to God creating them; therefore you are a human being. I can guarantee you that there are those who already have a name, a place and code for you, and the Almighty God is the only one who can and will break that code. What is this problem between African Americans and Whites that have caused conflict after conflict? This conflict has caused the most violent acts to be carried out upon (both African American and White) human beings, which I have seen even in my short life span. Conflict, violence, resolutions- What resolution(s) can we apply to the followings:

1) August 1995: Why would a police officer, as a witness for a high profile case purge himself by saying that he never used the "nigger word" in the last ten years? Los Angeles, California

2) July 1995: Why would a Governor of a State and the Regent Board vote against affirmative actions? California

3) July 1995: Why would a group of males hold a "White Male Only" gathering and have articles printed with the word "Nigger" on

it? Tennessee

4) June 1995: Why would five 18-year- old high school graduating White males spell out under their pictures in their year book "Kill all Niggers"! Connecticut

5) November 1994: Why would a political party orchestrate themselves so accurately until they seat enough persons in the House of Representative and the Senate to control Congress, to start at once repealing laws, but at the same time construct what they call "a contract with America" Washington, D.C.

6) October 1994: Why would a 23-year -old white mother drown her precious gifts from God (two sons), and say "A black man took my car with my babies and would not let me get them out." Union, South Carolina

7) June 1994: Why would an expert witness (White female) for a so-called "High Profile Case" in which the state never looked for any other suspect(s) use the word "Negroid" in answering the defense lawyer's question pertaining to "hair", and insist upon using it even after the lawyer tried to get her to say "African-American." "Negroid is written in

the manual, so this is what we have to use." Los Angeles, California

8) May 1994: Why would a principal (White) of high school try to keep white and African American couples from attending their high school prom, and tell a child of an African-American and White parent that she was a "mistake." Wedowee, Alabama

9) March 1992: Why would experienced police officers beat an African American man mercilessly (even the then President of the U.S. thought that it was wrong), and while doing such use the words "gorilla in the midst." California

10) July 1995: Why would a Baptist Convention pass a resolution apologizing to African-Americans about "slavery". Atlanta, Georgia

11) July 1994: Why would an eight year-old African-American male ask "Mommie, what is a Nigger?" When asked "Why are you asking me that question," one answer was "Well, sometimes when I am reading a book or watching a TV program about slaves, some White people use the word *nigger*, and sometimes I hear

some African-American people use the word *nigger* to each other."

So, here are six chapters of the Case (research) that we found out of my grandfather's trunk. We chose these six chapters (along with the suggested reading list) because we feel that you will gain enough information to understand the orgin of the "nigger word," what and who the "nigger word" is structered into, how to counter act the use of the "nigger word" by some toward others, and to help all of us to become "nigger word" literate. We have quoted word for word because we believe this is the conflict that has led to many of our problems here on American soil. We also believe that some are still studying this research in groups, and applying the structure to African-Americans in particular. The burning *why* questions in me did not rest until the Almighty God made me plan time to sit down and read the research all the way through carefully. His spirit directed me to pray to Him first, believe in Him, trust in Him, and not to be scared. He has everything under control. He sees and hears everything. He is in the midst of the secret meetings. He knows what the 50 niggerology classes curriculum are built on. (Niggerology is the study of and the application of niggerism), (Niggerism is the doctrine or theory that assume that the negro (African - African American) is sub-human). He is working out everything. Just you be careful that you do not cause yourself any problems. He will make the way for you to survive. If you make any mistakes, He will forgive you, but He can never change His laws or back up any lies.

We are asking you to be the juror, this case and write what you think each chapter was/is about. Let's discuss the research. I have not written in this research any of my opinions because I do not want to impose what I think upon you. I listed the why questions because these things actually happened. The Case (research) is open for discussion.

The World can label any other case/trial as the case/trial of the century, but the case (research) that you will be reading is The Case of the Centuries, and Africans - later African Americans have been on trial for over 400 years in these United States. Only the Almighty Judge can render the verdict (guilty or not guilty) and impose the sentence. This case is the foundation for the good, the bad and the ugly that all Americans have experienced for over 400 years. We will always love you, my brothers (African Americans and Whites), but we can never love some of your actions.

You see, when something comes up over and over again, it behooves someone to do research for the possible origin of that something. *"Nigger"*, Where did the word come from? Who birth the word? What does it mean and what is it based upon coming from those who birth the word? Was the word structured around and into a subject? Who was taught the "nigger word" subject? Why were they taught such? Has the "nigger word" subject affected anyone? - How? Will the niggerology (the study of niggerism) schools ever be dismantled?

THE CASE OF THE CENTURIES

Chapter I.
The Formation of the Negro and other Beasts-then Man on the Sixth Day.

There are just two schools of learning in the world to-day, which propose to explain the existence of the heavens and the earth, with all the phenomena which characterize each. These are (1) The Scriptural School of Divine Creation, (2) The Atheistic of Natural Development.

In discussing this subject Mr. Haeckel says: "As is now very generally acknowledged, both by the adherents of and the opponents of the theory of descent, the choice in the matter of the origin of the human race, lies between two radically different assumptions: We must either accustom ourselves to the idea that the various species of animals and plants, man included, originated independently of each other, by the supernatural process of a divine 'creation,' which as such is entirely removed from the sphere of

WHAT IS A NIGGER

scientific observation-or we are compelled to accept the theory of descent in its entirety, and trace the human race, equally with the various animals and plant species, from an entirely simple primeval parent form. Between these two assumptions there is no third course." -The Evolution of Man, Vol. II., pp, 36, 37.

The School of Creation teaches that the heaven and the earth, with all the phenomena which characterize each, is the product of divine creation. In direct opposition to this scriptural school, the School of Atheism teaches that the heaven and the earth, with all the phenomena which characterize each, is the result of natural causes working without design to accomplish their formation.

In our investigations, with a view to decide intelligently whether the phenomena of the universe is the product of divine creation, or whether it is the result of natural causes, we have three reliable guides to a correct decision. These are Science, Reason and Revelation.

Science teaches that the lowest element

THE CASE OF THE CENTURIES

of which it has any knowledge is matter. Science also teaches that matter exists in the material universe in just three forms, the solid, liquid and gasous. And inasmuch as all bodies, celestial and terrestial, are resolvable into matter in its gaseous state, science very property decides that matter in its gaseous state was the primitive condition of all bodies. Science also teaches that "matter is not self-existent."-*Guyot.* "Creation," appendix.

But to the question, from whence came matter? Science, which deals alone with second causes, gives no answer. But just at this point in our investigations, to which science leads us, and beyond which Science is powerless to guide us, reason comes to our assistance, with the assurance that, inasmuch as matter, is not self-existent, it must have been created. Hence, the very presence of matter, even in its primitive state, the gaseous, clearly demonstrates the exixtence of a Creator while its combination in all the varied forms, celetial and terrestrial, in which we find it to-day, bespeaks the most infinite

WHAT IS A NIGGER

design; and reason assures us that design can alone be formed and expressed by intelligence.

But to the question: "When and by whom was matter created?" Reason gives no answer, but just at this point in our investigation, to which Reason leads us, and beyond which Reason is powerless to guide us, and it would seem that any further advance that we may attempt must be merely speculative, revelation generously comes to our assistance with that sublime assurance that, "In the beginning God created the heaven and the earth."

Thus Revelation, in harmony with science, and with Reason, emphatically confirms the teachings of each, that there is a God; a personal God; a Creator, distinct from his creation; that there was a creation, and a clearly stated in the Mosaic Record, there was a definite plan of the creation; a creation sucessive-extending through "six days."

The initial step was the creation "in the beginning" of the lowest element-matter-as stated in the first verse; this followed in the second

THE CASE OF THE CENTURIES

verse by a correct description of matter in its primitive, or gaseous state, and this by the production of light-cosmic light-on the first day; continuing by the formation of the heavens on the second day; the separation of the "dry land" from the "waters" and the introduction of animal life in the fish, followed by the fowl on the fifth day; the bringing fourth of the cattle, creeping things, and beasts; the whole terminating in the creation of Man "in the image of God," on the sixth day.

We are thus enabled to realize "the necessity of a direct revelation of these great fundamental truths, to which human wisdom could not attain in any other way, which without the sanction of God's word were doomed to remain simple hypotheses, incapable of proof."-*Guyot*

"In the first verse we are taught that this universe had a beginning; that it was created-and that God was its Creator. The central idea is creation. The Hebrew word is bara, translated by create. It has been doubted whether the word

WHAT IS A NIGGER

meant a creation, in the sense that the world was not derived from any pre-existing material, nor from the substance of God Himself; but the manner in which it is here used does not seem to justify such a doubt. For whatever be the use of the word in other parts of the Bible, it is employed in this chapter in a discriminating way, which is very remarkable, and cannot but be intentional. Elsewhere, when only transformations are meant, as in the second and fourth days, or a continuation of the same kind of creation; as in the land animals of the fifth day, the word asah (maw) is used. Again, it is a significant fact that in the whole Bible where the simple form of bara is used it is always with reference to a work made by God, but never by man."-Ibid. pp. 29, 30, 31.

The Mosaic Record teaches that there is just three creations. The first of these is described in connection with "the heaven and the earth, in the beginning." The second creation is described in connection with the introduction of animal life on the fifth day; and the third creation is described in connection with the first appearance

THE CASE OF THE CENTURIES

of Man on the sixth day.

In order that we may properly appreciate the value of this scriptural teaching, we must first understand what constitutes a creation, as described in the Mosaic Record. This we understand to be the introduction into the material universe of some element, that had no prior existence there. This leads us to decide that, the remote past-in the beginning-what is now the material universe was empty space. This condition gave place to the creations, and formations described in the Record.

First, the creation of "the heaven and the earth," "in the beginning;" that is, the creation of matter, the material out of which "the heaven and the earth," with most of the phenomena which characterize each, were found.

That matter was the creation described in the first verse of the Mosaic Record, is clearly proven by the correct description of matter in its primitive or gaseous state, as given in the second verse of the records, as follows:

"And the earth was without form and void;

WHAT IS A NIGGER

and darkness was upon the face of the deep. And the Spirit of God moved upon the face of the waters."

Mr. Guyot says: "The matter just created was gaseous; it was without form, for the property of gas is to expand indefinitely. It was void, or empty, because, apparently, homogeneous and invisible. It was dark, because as yet inactive, light being the result of the action of physical and chemical forces not yet awakened. It was a deep, for its expansion in space, though indefinite, was not infinite, and it had dimensions. And the Spirit of God moved upon the face of that vast, inert, gaseous mass, ready to impart to it motion, and to direct all its subsequent activity, according to a plan gradually revealed by the works of the great cosmic days." Ibid. pp. 38.

We are thus enabled to recognize the broad distinction which the inspired author draws between creation and formation. A creation is the first introduction into the material universe of some element that had no prior existence there. A formation is something made out of

THE CASE OF THE CENTURIES

some pre-existing material; the result of a mere change wrought in the form of the original element.

"The era of progress opens with the first day's work. At God's command, movement begins, and the first result is the production of light. This was no creation, but a simple manifestation of the activity of matter; for, according to modern physics, heat and light are but different intensities of the vibratory motions of matter."-*Guyot*.

The production of the heavens on the second day, was not a creation, and is not described as such; they were simply formations our of the original creation, matter. The introduction of plant life on the third day was not a creation, and is not described as such. God simply commanded the earth to bring it forth. The luminaries which made their appearance on the fourth day, were not creations and are not so described; they were mere formations our of the original creation-matter.

From the creation of matter "in the

WHAT IS A NIGGER

beginning," throughout the first four days, the work of God was confined to the handling of matter. But the fifth day is distinguished from its predecessors by the introduction, that day, of a new element, which made its first appearance in the material universe in combination with matter, as presented in the physical organism of the fish, which is described as follows: "And God created the great stretched out sea monsters; and all living creatures that creep, which the waters breed abundantly after their kind."

It is the universal opinion of theologians, and of such scientists as accept the Bible as true, that this creation was that of animal life. To this view, which is at once opposed to the teachings of scripture and of science, we are compelled to dissent. Animal life is not a creation. Life itself is not a creation; neither plant life nor animal life; and it is not so described in the Mosaic Record.

Aside from the teachings of scripture and of science our personal observation teaches us that there is not such difference between plant

THE CASE OF THE CENTURIES

life and animal life as would justify us in deciding that plant life was merely a combination of the elements inherent in matter, and that animal life was a creation distinct from matter. Each has its germ, "containing the same elements in the same proportions." (Dana.) Each has its circulating fluid; each its forminative period; each its youth; each its maturity; each its decline and final dissolution. Mr. Dana says: "the vegetable and animal kingdoms are the opposite, but mutually dependent sides or parts of one system of life." (See Manual of Geology, p. 115). Hence, if life was a new element in the material universe, it would have been described as a creation, when plant life, which is merely "one side or part" of the "system," made its first appearance on the globe. But inasmuch as plant life, the first "side or part" of the "system," to make its appearance is not described as a creation it would be at once irrational, unscientific, and unscriptural, to decide that animal life the other "side or part" of "the system," which afterwards made its appearance, was a creation. In other words, if

WHAT IS A NIGGER

the "system of life" was a creation distinct from matter, it would have been so described at its first appearance in the plant.

The strength of our position is clearly demonstrated by the more detailed description of the subject given in the fourth and fifth verses of the second chapter of Genesis, as follows:

"These are the generations of the heavens and the earth, when they were created, in the day that the Lord God made the earth and the heavens; and every plant of the field before it was in the earth, and every herb of the field before it grew."

We are thus plainly taught, that the elements of plant life are simply parts of the original creation-matter. Hence, they existed in matter prior to the formation of matter into the earth. Thus by creating in matter the elements of life, "the Lord God" made "every plant of the field before it was in the earth, and every herb of the field before it grew."

Inasmuch as plant life and animal life are "mutual dependent sides or parts of one system of life," whose elements are identical, it follows,

THE CASE OF THE CENTURIES

that the elements of animal life, like those of plant life, were a part of the original creation-matter. And that they existed in matter prior to the formation of matter into the earth. Hence the combination of these original elements into plants and animals, and the first appearance of these on the globe in obedience to God's command, were not creations, and are not described as such in the Mosaic Record.

That the elements of life-both plant and animal life-were parts of the original creation-matter and that they existed in matter prior to the formation of matter into the earth, is further shown by the identity of language used by God in commanding the earth and the waters to bring forth plant and animal life, as follows:

"And God said, Let the earth bring forth grass, the herb yeilding seed, and the fruit tree yielding fruit after his kind, whose seed is in itself, upon the earth; and it was so.

"And God said, Let the waters bring forth abundantly the moving creatures that hath life."

"And God said, Let the earth bring forth

WHAT IS A NIGGER

the living creature after his kind; cattle, and creeping things, and beasts of the earth after his kind; and it was so. (See Gen. ii, 11, 20, 24).

What "was so"? Why, just as in deference to Divine will, the waters of the Red Sea parted, and stood mountain high on either side, while Israel passed "dry shod," so, in obedience to divine command did the earth and the waters combine the elements of plant and animal life, and "bring forth" plants and animals "after his kind."

Since the "system of life is not a creation, what new element described as a creation made its appearance on the fifth day, in combination with matter as pesented in the physical organism of the fish? To answer this question intelligently we must first ascertain what character pre-eminently distinguishes not only the highest but the lowest order of animals from the plant.

Mr. Dana says; "Plants have no consciousness of self, or of other existences; animals are conscious of an outer world, and even the lowest show it by avoiding obstacles."

THE CASE OF THE CENTURIES

-Ibid, p. 116.

The physical organism of the fish was simply a combination of elements of matter. But consciousness, which made its first appearance in the material universe on the fifth day, was an element distinct from matter. It was not present in light, nor in the heavens, nor in the plants, nor in the luminaries. It was a new element. Hence it is properly described as a creation.

What is consciousness? Mr. Webster defines it as "The knowledge of sensations, or of what passes in one's own mind." In support of this, he refers to Locke, Reid, and the encyclopedias. (See Unabridged Dictionary.) A moment's reflection should convince us that mind is an element distinct from matter.

Since consciousness is always associated with mind, and is never found in separation from it, we must decide that it is one of its attributes; and that its presence clearly demonstrates the existence of mind. Hence this new element, described as a creation which made its appearance

WHAT IS A NIGGER

in the material universe on the fifth day, in combination with matter as presented in the physical structure of the lowest order of animal- the fish-was mind, in its simplest form.

From the introduction of the fish, God handles this combination of matter and mind on up through the different grades of animals until the creation of man. The evidence of this is found in the fact that, though the higher orders of fowls and beasts possess more highly developed physical and mental structures than the fish, the difference between them is merely one of degree. They present no new element, but, like the fish, are simply a combination of matter and mind. Hence, they are not described as creations.

The belief is widely diseminated that mind is peculiar to man. Hence, man alone possesses the faculty of reason; and that the lower animals possess mere intinct. The fallacy of this belief has long since been demonstrated. Mr. Darwin says: "Of all the faculties of the human mind, it will, I presume, be admitted that reason stands at the summit. Only a few persons now dispute that

THE CASE OF CENTURIES

animals possess some power of reasoning. Animals may constantly be seen to pause, deliberate, and resolve. It is a significant fact that the more the habits of any animal are studied by a naturalist, the more he attributes to reason and the less to unlearned instincts." For futher information of the existence of mind, and the display of its various attributes in the fish and fowl and beast, see the works of Curvier, Darwin, Quatrefages, Hartman and others.

When the fish and fowl and beast were all made after their kind, God then said, "Let us make man in our own image after our likness. * * * So God created man in his own image, in the image of God created he him; male and female created he them."-Gen. i, 26-27.

In the more detailed description of the creation of man given in the 2d chapter of Genesis, verse 7, we are taught that "The Lord God formed man out of the dust of the ground, and breathed into his nostrils the breath of life; and man became a living soul." "The dust of the ground," "out" of which "The Lord God formed

WHAT IS A NIGGER

man." was part of the original creation-matter. We are thus plainly taught that the physical structure of man was simply a formation out of matter; and like the fish and fowl and beast, man received his animal life from matter. Hence, when his physical and mental organisms were completed, man, like the lower animals, was simply a combination of matter and mind.

Geological research demonstrates that death-physical death-entered the world almost simultaneously with life plant life. And that it followed closely upon the introduction of animal life. Since man, like the lower animals derived his animal life from matter, it follows that his physical and mental organisms, like theirs, must be subject to accident, disease, decay, and final dissolution. Hence, the idea that Adam would have lived on indefinitely, and perhaps never have experienced physical death, had he not violated Divine law, is too absurd for serious consideration. Man like the lower orders of animal life and like the plants has his germ, his formative period, his youth, his maturity, his

THE CASE OF THE CENTURIES

decline, and his physical dissolution.

"The breath of life" which God "breathed into" man's "nostrils" was spiritual, immortal life; life which, like God's life, never dies; "and man became a living soul." This spiritual, immortal life-this living soul-was a new element in the material universe. Hence, man, with whose physical and mental structure it was combined, is properly described as a creation.

Thus, the three creations-matter, mind and spiritual life-were combined in man; that sublime creature whom God honored in the creation by the bestowal of his likeness and his image, and to whom he confided dominion over the works of his hands. Well might David exclaim in describing God's creation of man: "Thou mad'st him a little lower than the angels, and has crowned him with glory and honor."

In obedience to Divine command, the waters and the earth brought forth the fish and fowl and beast after their kind. But God created man in his own image, upon a plan carefully matured and as carefully preserved in his "book."

WHAT IS A NIGGER

Well may we exclaim in the language of the Psalmist: "I will praise thee, for I am fearfully and wonderfully made; marvelous are thy works; and that my soul knoweth right well. My substance was not hid from thee when I was made in
secret and curiously wrought in the lowest parts of the earth. Thine eyes did see my substance, yet being imperfect; and in thy book all my members were written, which in continuance were fashioned, when as yet there was none of them."-Ps. cxxxix.

Prior to the creation of man, there was no link, no tie of kinship between the creator and his creation. But when "the Lord God formed man out of the dust of the ground," this "dust of the ground" being a part of the original creation-matter-and "breathed into his nostrils the breath of life"-spiritual, immortal life-man became "a living soul." This spiritual, immortal life, this living soul, was a part of the substance of God. Hence its combination with matter and with mind, as presented in Adam, formed the connecting

THE CASE OF THE CENTURIES

link, the link of kinship between creator and his creature. Thus, Adam became, literally and truly, as he is desribed in scripture, the son of God. (Luke iii, 38.) Adam was as literally and truly the son of God as was Isaac the son of Abraham. And the descendants of Adam, of pure Adamic stock, are sons and daughters of God, throughout all time, just as the descendants, of Abraham of pure Abrahamic stock are sons and daughters of Abraham throughout all time. But in drawing this comparison we should be careful not to confound processes with results. The combination of spiritual, immortal life-a living soul-itself a part of the substance of God, with matter and with mind as presented in Adam's physical, mental and spiritual organisms, was the result of a creative act of the creator; while the presence of these characteristic in Isaac, himself a descendant of Adam, was the result of a generative act of the creature.

Further evidence that Adam was the son of God is found in the fact that when our saviour was on earth he recognized the pure-blooded

WHAT IS A NIGGER

descendants of Adam as his brethren and sisters. (See Matt. xii. 49; also Mark iii, 35.)

The completion of the life system of man, by the creation of the female, did not immediately follow that of the male. We are taught that "the Lord God planted a garden eastward in Eden; and there he put the man whom he had formed." (See Gen. ii.:8.) What period of time intervened between the creation of man and that of woman we have no means of ascertaining. However, we are led to decide that it was one of considerable length; for it was in this interval that "Adam gave names to all cattle, and to the fowl of the air, and to every beast of the field." (See Gen. ii.:20). The successful accomplishment of this great task, requiring the highest intelligence and the finest discriminating power, would have been creditable to a Cuvier or a Darwin. Hence, Adam's successful accomplishment of it clearly demonstrates his towering intellectuality.

In this early dawn of Adamic history, the great Architect of the universe looked out upon his yet unfinished creation and said: "It is not

THE CASE OF THE CENTURIES

good that man should be alone; I will make him a helpmeet for him.

* * * And the Lord God caused a deep sleep to fall upon Adam, and he slept; and he took one of his ribs, and closed up the flesh instead thereof. And the rib, which the Lord God had taken from man, made he a woman, and brought her unto the man."

We of modern times are wont to boast our greater enlightenment as compared with that of preceding ages; and as an evidence of it we proudly point to the sacredness of marriage, woman's honorable position, and her higher education. But a glimpse of very ancient history suffices to convince us that this is but a reformatory movement, indicating a disposition to return to primitive conditions. Among the Toltecs, who developed one of the great civilzations of America in ancient times, "the position of woman was honorable." Among the Aryans, who thousands of years ago developed the splendid civilization of ancient India, "woman was held in respect, and marriage was sacred."

WHAT IS A NIGGER

And there are beautiful hymns in existence today which were composed and written by the ladies and queens of Aryans.

When we trace to its fountain source this elevated, ennobling character in man, his respectful devotion to woman, it leads us to the creation. This noble character found its first expression in the first recorded utterance of Adam, upon his reception of that lovely helpmeet whom God had made for him. "This is now bone of my bones, and flesh of my flesh; she shall be called woman, because she was taken out of man. Therefore shall a man leave his father and his mother and cleave unto his wife; and they shall be one flesh."

We would vainly search the annals of the world for a sentiment more chaste, more elevated, and more devotional than this, to the fair sex of our mother; not one of the gallant knights who wielded a lance in the age of chivalry ever gave expression to a sentiment
more chivalrous toward the lady of his choice, whose feelings and whose honor he stood pledged

THE CASE OF THE CENTURIES

to defend with his life.

Man, the male, and woman, the female, are "the opposite but mutually dependent sides or parts" of the spiritual life system of the globe; and the presence of each is essential to the existence and perpetuation of the system. Hence, "it is not good that man should be alone."

In addition to this, the presence of woman has exerted a beneficial influence upon the man throughout the ages that have passed. All history, sacred and profane, and all tradition, ancient and modern, and all observation and experience combine to teach us:

> "That man is the cloud of coming storm,
> Dark as the raven's murky plume,
> Save where the sunbeams light and warm
> Of woman's soul and woman's form
> Gleams brightly o'er the gath'ring gloom."

While in all that is angelic, woman stands peerless in the realm of created things. And when we'd seek some symbol of her, even in the floral kingdom, that wondrous exhibition of the most exquisite taste, displayed by the great Artist of the universe, we find perhaps her fittest symbol

WHAT IS A NIGGER

in that matchless combination of beauty and fragrance, the night-blooming cereus, which, while generously contributing its odors to enrich the world's wealth of fragrance, modestly conceals its beauties 'neath the veil of night.

Thus it is shown that man is a creation as separate and distinct from the fish and fowl and beast as he is from the plant or the planet. Hence, we might with just as much propriety consider him simply a member of the animal kingdom. It would be no more irrational, no more unscientific, if you please, and certainly no more unscriptural, to consider man an undeveloped planet than to consider him merely "a highly developed animal."

In harmony with the teachings of the Mosiac Record, St. Paul says: "All flesh is not the same flesh: but there is one kind of flesh of men, another flesh of beasts, another of fishes, and another of birds." (See I Cor. xv. 39,) Since there are four different kinds of flesh, each separate and distinct from the others, it follows that even the flesh of man is a "kind of flesh"

THE CASE OF THE CENTURIES

distinct from that of the fish or fowl or beast. Hence we are emphatically taught that there is no kinship between man and the animals; but that the kinship is between God and man.

We should also note the broad distinction in point of numbers and variety which God made in the creation between the representatives of the spirtual life of the globe, as presented in man, and the representatives of mere animal life, and those of plant life. The plants and the fish and fowl and beast were all made in great numbers and in great variety. While there are such resemblances between certain plants, and between certain animals, as justifies the naturalist in deciding that they are of the same family or species, there are such differences between certain members of these families or species as justifies the naturalist in deciding that they are different races. These, whether of plant or fish or fowl or beast, were all made after their kind. But not so with man. Man was not made after any kind, but was created "in the image of God." Neither was man made in great numbers and

WHAT IS A NIGGER

varieties, but was created a single pair. Hence, unlike the plants and fish and fowl and beast, man was not made in species and races, but is a distinct creation. Had God desired man, like the plants and animals, to be a species, divisible into races, no good reason could be advanced as to why he did not so create them. Had there been a plurality of gods, man would have been created a species, comprising a greater or less number of men; and this species of man would have been divided into different races of men, each of whose racial characters would have corresponded with the characters of the god in whose image they were made. But, inasmuch as there is only one God, so was there created in his image just one man, whom he called "Adam, the son of God." And not only is man distinguished from the mere animals by his possession of spiritual, immortal life-a living soul, itself a part of the substance of God-but even his flesh is a different kind of flesh from that of the fish or fowl or beast. (See I. Cor. xv, 39.) And when, in order that the Adamic creation should be enabled to

THE CASE OF THE CENTURIES

perpetuate its existence, and increase its numbers on earth, God decided to "make a helpmeet" for Adam, it is significant that he made the female man out of the male man. Thus completed and perfected by the presence of woman, it was possible for man to beget offspring, to whom he would transmit his physical, mental and spiritual characters, and be thus enabled to excute those divine
laws: "Be fruitful and multiply, and replenish the earth and subdue it; and have dominion over the fish of the sea, and over the fowl of the air, and over every living thing that moveth upon the earth." (Gen. i, 28.)

Inasmuch as man was created the son of God, was made "a little lower than the angels," and was assigned to dominion over the works of God's hands, it follows that he is not a development from a lower form; and it also follows that he could never develop into a higher or more perfect form while he lived on the earth.

In this professedly Christian age we hear much of a "human species" which is divisible

WHAT IS A NIGGER

into "races of men." In view of the plain teaching of the Bible that man is a distinct creation, it is pertinent to inquire where the modern world obtained this absurd idea that man is a "species" which is divisible into "races of men"-from the scriptures? We have vainly sought from Genesis to Revelation for the slightest hint of the existence of such a thing as a "human species" or a "race of men."

The terms "species" and "races" are scientific terms; they belong to natural science, and are used to describe what is termed "natural relations." But the
terms "human species" and "races of men" belong exclusively to the atheistic school of Natural Development, which teaches that man is a highly developed species of ape-the human species-and that this human species of ape is divisible into five or more "races of men." On the other hand, the terms "tribes," "nations" and "empires" are political terms, and are used to describe political relations. And it is a significant fact, and one which the professed Christian would do well to

THE CASE OF THE CENTURIES

observe, that these political terms-tribes, nations and empires-are invariably employed by the inspired authors in describing the relations of men. The terms "human species" and "races of men" are conspicuous in scripture by their absence.

The first reference to the "races of men" which we find in ancient history is found in the fragment of Plato's history of the lost continent of Atlantis. Plato lived 300 years B. C. He was the descendant of Solon, the great lawgiver of Athens. Solon spent ten years of his life in Egypt. In his discussions with the Egyptian priests Solon first heard of Atlantis and of the records concerning it to be found in the sacred registers of Egypt. Permission having been granted to examine them, Solon obtained from the sacred registers the necessary data from which to write in Greek a history of Atlantis. But before completing his work, Solon died. It seems that in the course of time his data or his manuscript fell into the hands of Plato, who decided to write a history of Atlantis. But after

WHAT IS A NIGGER

writing a description of the continent, its population, products, religion, wealth, culture, power, etc., Plato died, leaving a mere fragment of what, if completed, would have been one of the most invaluable contributions to the literature of the world.

The sacred registers of Egypt from which the data of Plato's history of Atlantis were obtained were far more ancient than the Bible. They were so much more ancient than any historical records of the Greeks, that any historical records of the Greeks, that an Egyptian priest said to Solon, "You have no antiquity of history, and no history of antiquity." Throughtout Plato's narrative frequent allusion is made to "the human race" and to the "race of men." These atheistic terms could only have originated in the atheistic school of evolution. And they are always employed by the advocates of the theory of man's descent from the ape. The presence of these terms in the sacred registers of ancient Egypt clearly indicates that "The Theory of Descent" was universally taught in perhaps as

THE CASE OF THE CENTURIES

systematized and elaborated a form in that remote period as it is in our day. And that in the dark ages which followed the crucifixion of the Saviour, this theory, in its systematized, elaborated form, in common with all literature, art, and science, was lost amid the crash of falling empires. But unfortunately the pernicious influences of this infamous theory upon the minds of men, together with its atheistic terms, survived its literature, and was handed down in a traditional way from generation to generation.

Thus we find that the "Theory of Descent," so far from being a product of the Christian era, was an old, demoralizing, degrading theory at the advent of our saviour. And that so far from its having been first outlined by Linnaeus, or Lamark, or Blumenbach, or to whomsoever belongs the discredit, and more recently systematized and elaborated by Darwin and his disciples, it actually antedates the Christian era thousands of years. It was the pernicious influence of this atheistic theory which was advocated by the idolatrous authors who lived

WHAT IS A NIGGER

and taught prior to the advent of the Saviour which so demoralized and degraded man and removed him so far from his God as to necessitate the sacrifice of the Son of God to redeem him.

Upon the revival of learning in modern time, the theory of evolution was again systematized, and is now as universally disseminated among men as it was in ancient time.

But who are they, and to what school do they belong, who would teach us that man is merely an animal and must take his position in "the zoological system" with the rest of the animals; that man is simply a highly developed species of ape- "the human species "-and that this "human species" of ape is divisible into five "races of men"-the Negro, the Malay, the Indian, the Mongolian, and the Caucasian? Darwin, Haeckel, Huxley, Tyndall, Spencer, Voltaire, and their disciples; that class of philosophers who would teach us the existence of a universe without a God, a creation without a Creator, man without religion, and the world without a Sabbath

THE CASE OF THE CENTURIES

or a Bible.

How do these philosophers treat God's word, which the devotees of "enlightened Christianity" profess to so much revere? Ordinarily, in attempting to explain the existence of "the heaven and the earth," with all the phenomena which characterize each, they make no reference to scripture, but treat it with silent contempt. The Bible occupies no place in their theory.

But when compelled to alude to it from any cause, they denounce it as a Semitic myth, a Hebrew legend, or a jewish tradition.

Further evidence of the antiquity of "The Theory of Descent," and of its prevalence in the days of the Apostles, is shown by the great opposing declaration of St. Paul that "all flesh is not the same flesh; but there is one kind of flesh is not the same flesh; but there is one kind of flesh of men, another flesh of beasts, another of fishes, and another of birds." A careful comparison of this teaching with that of "The Theory of Development" must convince us that

WHAT IS A NIGGER

this inspired declaration was a blow aimed directly at "The Theroy of Development," which teaches that the most complex organism is merely a development from the most simple. Hence, "all flesh" is akin.

What is most directly opposed to the inspired declaration of the great apostle that "all flesh is not the same flesh?" Necessarily we must decide that it is the theory that all flesh is the same flesh. What theory is this? It is the theory which teaches that animal life originated in the monera by "spontaneous generation" out of simple compounds of carbon, oxygen, hydrogen, and nitrogen." And that from this little monera, the lowest form of animal life, on up to and including man, all flesh is the same. It is the theory which teaches, in direct opposition to the Bible, that man is merely a highly developed species of ape-the "human species"- and that this "human species" of ape is divible into "five races of men." It is the Theory of Development.

What is most directly opposed to the

THE CASE OF THE CENTURIES

inspired declaration of the great apostle that "there is one kind of flesh of men, another flesh of beasts, another of fishes, and another of birds, making in all four different kinds of flesh, as separate and distinct from each other as if the one made its first appearance upon and inhabited the earth, the other the Moon, the other Jupiter, and the other Mars? Necessarily we must decide that it is the theory which teaches that, from the little monera on up to and including man, there is just one flesh in different stages of development. It is the Theory of Development.

How do you professed believers in God's word-you professed followers of the Saviour-you professed admirers of St. Paul-how do you treat this atheistic theory which god did all in his power, short of physical force, even to the sacrifice of his Son, to blot from the face of the earth; this infamous theory which Christ died to obliterate from the minds of men; this blasphemous theory which St. Paul, with his accustomed force and skill, dealt what will yet prove its death blow? How do you professed

WHAT IS A NIGGER

Christians treat this ante-scriptural theory that man is merely a highly developed species of ape-the "human species"-and that this "human species" is divisible into five "races of men"-the Negro, the Malay, the Indian, the Mongolian, and the Caucasian? You teach it at your fireside, you teach it in the social circle, you teach it on the highways and on the by-ways, you teach it in the kindergarten, you teach it in the Sabbath school, you teach it in your higher institutions of learning, you teach it through the press, you teach it from the lecture platform, and Oh! blasphem of blasphemies! you teach it at the altar!

And what is the result? To say nothing of the disastrous results which must inevitably accrue to you in eternity from your adherence to and your promulgation of this infamous theory in every relation in life from the cradle to the grave, what is the result to you in time? With those Divine promises ever held out imploringly to you-"Ask and ye shall receive," "and no good thing will he withhold from those who walk up

THE CASE OF THE CENTURIES

rightly;" you pray for a rain, and you get a drouth; you pray for fair weather, and you get a flood; you pray for prosperity, and want stares you in the face; you pray for happiness, and wretchedness and misery and degradation and disappointment and grief are your constant companions from the cradle to the grave; you pray for peace, and you get a war. Is god unable or unwilling to redeem his promises, or do you fail to walk uprightly?

It cannot be disproven that the theory now universally taught that man is a "species" divisible into "races" is an inseparable part of the theory of man's descent from the ape. Neither can it be denied that it is directly opposed to the plain teaching of the Bible that man, unlike the fish and fowl and beast, was created a single pair; hence, is not divisible into "species" and "races." The effort of modern Christianity to mix this atheistic theory that man is a "species" divisible into "races" with the scriptural teaching that man is a distinct creation, "in the image of God," must prove disastrous both in time and in

WHAT IS A NIGGER

eternity. Take any two different elements and mix them, and the product is neither the one nor the other of the originals; each of the originals in theory purity no longer exists; and the product resulting from their mixture is merely a compound in which is blended the characters peculiar to each. So it is in this case. The teachings of the Bible that man is a distinct creation, "in the image of God," and the theory that man is a "species of ape divisible into races of men" are opposites. Hence, the effort of professed Christians to mix the two has resulted in the destruction of Christianity from the earth; and also the destruction of the theory of Natural Development, to the extent to which it has been mixed with scripture. The theory of Natural Development in its purity is only found among those who reject the Bible in its entirely. And pure Christianity will never again shed its radiance upon man's pathway to the grave until the church as an organization, and each individual member of it utterly repudiates the atheistic theory of Natural Development, with all its

THE CASE OF THE CENTURIES

demoralizing teachings, its degrading influences, and its misleading terms.

Man alone was created "in the image of God;" the fish and fowl and beast, like the plants, were made after their kins. Man alone is responsible to God for his acts; the lower animals are responsible to man, under whose "dominion" they were placed in the creation, and into whose "hands" God delivered them after their preservation form the deluge. Man alone in his "first estate" was clothed with Divine authority to "have dominion" and he alone fell from this high "estate" by his wanton violation of Divine law. Hence, man alone is the subject of redemption.

Man was created "in the image of God"- male and female-a single pair-distinct from the fish and fowl and beast, which. like the plants, were made after their kind. This is the teaching of the scriptural narrative of Divine creation.

Man is a highly developed species of ape- the human species-and this human species is divisible into five races of men-the Negro, the

WHAT IS A NIGGER

Malay, the Indian, the Mongolian, and the Caucasian. This is the teachings of the atheistic theory of Natural Development, which thrusts God aside and declares that man, the most simple. Hence, according to this theory, man traces his pedigree back through the beast and fowl and fish to the lowest form of animal.

The absolute conflict between the teachings of these opposing schools-Divine Creation and Natural Development-is apparent. Hence, if that most complex organism, man, is merely a development from the most simple; if he has descended from the ape, and is simply a highly developed species of ape-the human species-and this "human species" is divisible into five "races of men," it follows that he was not created "in the image of God"-a single pair- and his flesh is not, as Paul tells us, a different kind of flesh from that of the fish and fowl and beast, but is akin to it.

If, on the other hand, that most complex organism, man, was created "in the image of God"-a single pair-and if, as Paul tell us, his

THE CASE OF THE CENTURIES

flesh is a different kind of flesh from that of the fish and fowl and beast, then he is not a development from the most simple organism, and there is no kinship between man and the animals.

Let us now compare the teachings of the gospel with reference to the origin and mission of the Saviour and the ultimate basis of the gospel, with the teaching of the modern christian church upon this subject, and the ultimate basis of the church.

We are taught by the gospel that Jesus Christ was the Son of God, and that he came into the world and suffered and died to redeem fallen man. What is the ultimate basis of this teaching? The narrative of Divine creation, which teaches that man was "created" "in the image of God"-a single pair-distinct from the fish and fowl and beast, which, like the plants, were made after their kind. (St. John i.)

In apparent harmony with the teaching of the gospel, the modern Christian church teaches that Jesus Christ was the son of God; and that he

WHAT IS A NIGGER

came into the world and suffered and died to redeem fallen man. But what is the ultimate basis of this teaching of the modern Christian church? The theory that man is a species (and of course if he is a species of anything, he is a species of ape)-the human species-and that this human species is divisible into five races of men-the Negro, the Malay, the Indian, the Mongolian, and the Caucasian. Thus it cannot be disproven that the teachings of the modern Christian church find their ultimate basis, not on the scriptural narrative of Divine creation, but upon the atheistic theory of Natural Development.

Evidently the church which Jesus Christ established on the narrative of Divine creation has been transferred to the theroy of Natural Development. Surely nothing could be more absurd, nothing more blasphemous than the attempt on the part of professed Christians to confuse the teachings and terms of these opposing schools.

The product resulting from the mixture of the teachings of these opposing schools is what

THE CASE OF THE CENTURIES

its devotees are pleased to term "Enlightened Christianity." But a glance at its atheistic teachings, its degrading influences, and its misleading terms, suffice to convince us that it is merely a counterfeit, in which is blended and distorted the teachings peculiar to scripture with those peculiar to atheism. Enlightened Christianity, indeed! How enlightened, and enlightening, is this modern Christianity which, under the influence of the atheistic theory of Natural Development, upon which it is based, ignores the broad distinction which God made in the creation between man and the ape, and places them in the same family as different races of one species of animal.

WHAT IS A NIGGER

Chapter II.
Biblical and Scientific Facts Demonstrating that the Negro is not an Offspring of the Adamic Family.

The White, the highest, and the Negro the lowest of the so-called "five races of men," present the strongest contrast to each other in their physical and mental characters; and in their modes of life, habits, customs, language, manners, gestures, etc.

White is not a color; neither is black a color; yet the white, colorless complexion of the white, finds its strongest contrast in the black, colorless complexion of the Negro.

The long, fine silken hair of the White, finds its strongest contrast in the short, coarse, woolly hair of the Negro. Each individual hair of the white "is cylindrical." Hence, "its section is circular." In striking contrast to that of the white, each individual hair of the Negro "is flattened like a tape." Hence, its section is oval." (Haeckel, Hist. of creation, vol. 11, pp.

THE CASE OF THE CENTURIES

414, 415.)

The relatively short, broad skull of the White, finds its strongest contrast in the long, narrow skull of the Negro. This length and narrowness of the Negro's skull is a character of the ape. Winchell says, "A certain relative width of skull appears to be connected with energy, force, and executive ability." Hence the narrowness of the Negro's skull denotes his lack of energy, force, and executive ability. This is significant, when considered in connection with the design of God in creating man, and the great task to which he was assigned in the Creation. Winchell quoting from the measurements of Broca says, (1) "The face of the Negro occupies the greater portion of the total length of the head. (2) His anterior cranium is less developed than his posterior, relatively to that of the White. (3) His occipital foramen is situated more backward in relation in relation to the total projection of the head, but more forward in relation to the cranium only. In other words, the Negro has the cerebral cranium less developed than the white;

WHAT IS A NIGGER

but its posterior is more developed than the anterior." (*Preademites*, pp. 169, 170.) "In the Negro skull the sphenoid does not, generally, reach the parietals, the coronal suture joining the margin of the temporals. The skull is very thick and solid, and is often used for butting, as is the custom of rams. It is flattened on the top, and well adapted for carrying burdens." (*Ibid*, p. 171.) The cephalic index * * * among Noachitis (whites), ranges from 75 to 83 degrees; among negroes, from 71 to 76 degrees. (*Ibid*, p. 246.)

In discussing cranial capacity, Dr. Winchell says, "Capacity of cranium is universally recognized as a criterion of psychic power. No fact is better established than the general relation of intellect to weight of brain. Welker has shown that the brains of twenty-six men of high intellectual rank surpassed the average weight by fourteen per cent. Of course quality of brain is an equally important factor; and hence not a few men with brains even below the average have distinguished themselves for scholarship and executive ability. The Noachites

THE CASE OF THE CENTURIES

possess a mean capacity of 1,500 cubic centimeters. * * * Among Negroes, 1,360 cubic centimeters." (*Ibid*, p. 246.)

"The average weight of the European brain, males and females, is 1340 grammes; that of the Negro is 1178; of the Hottentot, 974, and of the Australian, 907. The significance of these comparisons appears when we learn that Broca, the most eminent of French anthropologists, states that when the European brain falls below 978 grammes (mean of males and females), the result is idiocy. In this opinion Thurman coincides. The color of the Negro brain is darker than that of the White, and its density and texture are inferior. The convolutions are fewer and more simple, and, Agassiz and others long ago pointed out, approximate those of the quadrumama. (*Ibid*, pp. 249, 251.)

The atheism, which for ages has enveloped the world in darkness, erroneously teaches that all bipeds, with articulate speech, the erect posture, a well developed hand and foot, and the ability to make and handle tools, are men. Hence,

WHAT IS A NIGGER

no table exists, in which the average brain weight of the adult male, of pure Adamic stock is given. But, we feel assured, that this average may safely be placed at not less than 1,500 grammes. Winchell, Topinard, Quatrefages, and other scientists give the following table of "comparative weights of brains compiled from observations collected by Sanford B. Hunt, made during the civil was in the United States."

"State of hybridization.	Wt. of Brain. Grammes.
24 Whites	1,424
25 three parts white	1,390
47 half-white or mulattoes	1,334
51 one-quarter white	1,319
95 one-eighth white	1,308
22 one-sixteenth white	1,280
141 pure Negroes	1,331"

(Anthropology)

Had these estimates extended to every class of people in the United States the average

THE CASE OF THE CENTURIES

of whites would doubtless have been raised to 1,500 grammes. This average is far exceeded, by many individual whites; for example:

                          Weight of brain.
                          grms. oz.
Cuvier-63 years old-Naturalist..........1829.96 (64.54)
Byron-36 years old-Poet 1897.00 (63.73)
Lejisene Dirichlet-50 years-Mathe-matician....1520.00 (53.61)
(Quatrefages, *Human Species*, p. 411.)

In the table from which the above weights were taken, the brain weight of several distinguished individuals are given which fall below the average. This indicates that the weight and volume of the brain, is not the only factor to be considered in determining the relative intelligence of individuals. Quatrefages, while admitting "that there is a certain relation bewteen the development of the intelligence and the volume and weight of the brain," says, "But, at the same time, we must allow that the material

WHAT IS A NIGGER

element, that which is appreciable to our senses, is not the only one which we must take into account, for behind it lies hidden an unknown quantity an x, at present undetermined and only recognizable by its effects." (Ibid, p. 413.) This is a truth which is easily demonstrated by comparing the achievements of the white, with those of the Negro, and the mixed-bloods.

The relatively short, narrow jaw of the White finds its strongest contrast in the long, broad jaw of the Negro. This is another character of the ape which the Negro presents. The jaws of the Negro, like those of the lower apes, "extend forward at the expense of the symmetry of the face, and backward at the expense of the brain cavity." Quartrefages, says: "It is well known that in the Negro, the entire face, and especially the lower portion, projects forward. In the living subject it is exaggerated by the thickness of the lips. But it is also apparent in the skull, and constitutes one of its most striking characters." It is this trait which is opposed to the orthognathism of the White. (*Ibid*, p.p. 390, 391.)

THE CASE OF THE CENTURIES

Dr. Winchell says, "The amount of prognathism is another marked criterion of organic rank. One method of expressing this is by means of 'auricular radii,' or distances from the opening of the ear to the roots of the teeth, and to other parts of the head. Among Europeans, the distance to the base of the upper incisors is 99, but among negroes it averages 114. On the contrary, the average distance to the top of the head is, among Europeans, 112; but among negroes, 110. The distance to the upper edge of the occipital bone is, among Europeans, 104; among negroes, 104. The measurements prove that the Negro possesses more face, and particularly of jaws, and less brain above. Other measurements furnish a similar result; and show, also, that the development of the posterior brain, in relation to the anterior, is greater in the Negro. Prognathism is otherwise expressed by means of the 'facial angle,' or general slope of the face from the forehead to the jaws, when compared with a horizontal plane. Among the Noachites, the more face, and particularly of jaws, and less

WHAT IS A NIGGER

brain above. Other measurements prove that the facial line is nearest perpendicular, giving an angle of 77 degrees to 81 degrees. Among negroes, it averages only 67 degrees." (*Preademites*, p. 247.)

The prominent chin of the White finds its strongest contrast in the retreating chin of the Negro. This is another character of the ape which the Negro presents. Winchell says, "The retreating contour of the chin as compared with the European, approximates the Negro to the chimpanzee and lower mammals." (Ibid, p. 251.)

The front teeth of the White, set perpendicularly in the jaw, find their strongest contrast in the front teeth of the Negro, which set slanting in the jaw. This is another character of the ape which the Negro presents. Haeckel describes as Prognathi those "whose jaws, like those of the animal snout, strongly project, and whose front teeth, therefore, slope in front; and men with straight teeth Orthognathi, whose jaws project but little and whose front teeth stand perpendicularly."

THE CASE OF THE CENTURIES

The relatively thin lips of the White find their strongest contrast in the thick, puffed lips of the Negro. This is another character of the ape which the Negro presents. In referring to the differences presented by the mouth, in the so-called races of men, Quatrefages says, "The thousand differences of form and dimensions which exhibit, from the Negro of Guina with his enormous and, as it were, turned-up lips, to certain Aryan or Semitic whites can neither be measured nor described. * * * 'It may, however, be remarkd, that the thickness of the lips is very marked in all negroes, in consequence of their projection in front of the maxillary bones and the teeth. The mouth of the Negro presents another character which seems to me to have been generally neglected, and which has always struck me. It is a kind of clamminess at the outer border of the commissures, and seems to prevent the small movements of the corner of the mouth which play such an important part in the physiognomy. The dissections of M. Hamy have explained these facts. They have shown that in

WHAT IS A NIGGER

the negroes the muscles of this region are both more developed and less distinct than in the whites." (*The Human Species*, p. 367.)

The prominent nose of the White finds its strongest contrast in the flat nose of the Negro, which has the appearance of having been crushed in. This is another character of the ape which the Negro presents.

In contrasting the Negro skull and face with those of the White, Topinard says, "The Norman verticalis is of an elliptical shape. The supra-iniac portion of the occipital is frequently projecting, its portions are flat and vertical, the curved temporal lines describe an arc corresponding with the mass of temporal muscles which are inserted beneath them; the temporal shell itself is longer than that of the White. the frontal is articulated frequently with the temporal; the greater wings of the sphenoid are consequently not articulated with the parietal. The cranial sutures are more simple than in the white type, and are obliterated sooner (Gratiolet). The squamo-temporal and the spheno-parietal

THE CASE OF THE CENTURIES

frequently form a horizontal straight line. The forehead is narrow at the base, sometimes receding and rather low, sometimes straight and bulging (bombe) at the summit. The frontal bosses are often confluent, or replaced by a single and median protuberance. * * * 'The orbits, moreover, are microsemes, that is to say, short from above downwards. * * * 'The eyeballs are close to the head, and the palpebral apertures are nevertheless small and are on the same horizontal line. * * * 'The nose is developed in width at the expense of its projection; its base is larger and crushed in, owing to the softness of the cartilages, and spreads out into two divergent alae, with elliptical nostrils more or less exposed. This extremity is sometimes tri-lobed. The skelton of the nose is platyrrhinian (54-78); the two bones proper are occasionally united, as in apes. * * * The prognathism of the Negro extends within certain limits to the entire face. All the parts of the superior maxilla contribute to it, and even the pterygoid processes, which are drawn forward by the development of the jaw; but it is

WHAT IS A NIGGER

only characteristic and considerable in the subnasal region and in the teeth. It frequently exists also in the lower jaw; that is to say, the chin recedes, and the teeth project obliquely forward. The teeth are wider apart than in the white races, beautifully white, very firm and sound. Lastly, the ears are small, round, their border not well curled, the lobule short and scarcely detached, and the auditory opening wide. The neck is short." (Anthropology, p.p. 488, 489, 490.)

The long, slender neck of the White finds its strongest contrast in the short, thick neck of the Negro. In this, the Negro presents another character of the ape. Burmeister, quoted by Hartman, says, "The negro's thick neck is the more striking, since it is generally allied with a short throat. In measuring negroes from the crown of the head to the shoulder, I found the interval to be from nine and a quarter to nine and three-quarters inches. In Europeans of normal height this interval is seldom less than ten inches, and is more commonly eleven inches in women

THE CASE OF THE CENTURIES

and twelve in men. The shortness of the neck, as well as the relatively small size of the brain-pan, and the large size of the face, may the more readily be taken as an approximation to the Simian type, since all apes are short-necked. * * * This shortness of the neck of the Negro explains his greater carrying power, and his preference for carrying burdens on his head, which is much more fatiguing to the European on account of his longer and weaker neck." (*Anthropoid Apes*, p.p. 100, 101.)

"The clavicle is longer in proportion to the hunmerus than in the White. His radius is perceptibly longer in proportion to the humerus-thus approximating to that of the ape. The scapular is shorter and broader. (*Preadimites*, p. 171.) "Among negroes the forearm is longer, in proportion to the arm, than is the case with whites. The same is true of anthropoid apes. The Negro's arm, when suspended by the side, reaches the knee-pan within a distance of only four and three-eighths per cent of the chole length of the body. The white man's arm reaches the knee-

WHAT IS A NIGGER

pan within a distance which is seven and one-half per cent of the whole length of the body. This length of the arm is a quadrumanous characteristic. (*Ibid*, p.p. 248, 249.) Topinard says, "The arm * * * is shortest in whites, longest in negroes. * * * Frequently, in the latter, the extremity of the middle finger touched the patella; once it was twelve millmeters below its upper border, as in the gorilla." (*Anthropology*, p. 335.) Quatrefages says, "I have already observed that the upper limb is a little longer in the Negro than in the White. The essential cause of this difference is the relative elongation of the forearm." M. Broca, after comparing the radius and humerus of the two races, gives 79.43 for the Negro, and 73.82 for the Europeans. (*The Human Species*, P. 399.)

Mr. Hartman says, "In the case of an adult male gorilla the first glance at this member reminds us of the knotty fist of a black laborer or lighterman, like those who, at Rio de Janeiro, Bahia, or La Guayra, lift the heavy bags of coffee and place them on their heads or on their

THE CASE OF THE CENTURIES

herculean shoulders." (*Anthropoid Apes*, p. 102.)

Winchell says, "Among the Negroes the capacity of the lungs is less than among the Whites; and the circumference of the chest is less." (*Preadimites*, p. 173.)

Quatrefages says, "The thoracic cage presents some interesting facts sufficiently well proved. In consequence of the form of the sternum, the greater or less curvation of the ribs, it is generally broad and flattened in the White, narrow and prominent in the Negro." (*The Human Species*, p. 397.)

Topinard says, "M. Pruner-Bey speaks of two important characters which remind one of the ape. The three curvatures of the spine are less pronounced in the Negro than in the White; his thorax is relatively flat from side to side, and slightly cylindrical. The shoulders, he adds, are less powerful than in the European. The umbilicus is nearer the pubis; the iliac bones in the male are thicker and more vertical. The neck of the femur is less oblique." (*Anthropology*, p. 490.)

WHAT IS A NIGGER

Topinard says, "The pelvis, formed by the two iliac bones and the sacrum, is divided into two parts-the great pelvis, or wide upper portion, and the small pelvis, or pelvis cavity, through which the fetus passes at birth. Camper and Soemmering observed that the pelvis of the Negro in its ensemble is narrower than that of the White.- 'In 1826 Vrolik came to the conclusion that the pelvis of the male negro-from its strength and thickness-from the want of transparency in its iliac fossoe-from the higher projection of its superior extremity, and from the spinous processes of the iliac bones being less projecting and less separated from the cotyloid cavities, approximates to that of animals, while the pelvis of the negress maintains a certain slenderness. In 1864 Joulin asserted that the transverse diameter of the inlet is always greater antero-posteriorly in the female.
* * * In the negress, he says, the iliac bones are more vertical, the transparency of the fossoe, the capacity and depth of the cavity less, the pubic arch, as well as its angle greater." (*Ibid*, pp. 305,

THE CASE OF THE CENTURIES

306.) "Weber found that in each of the races which he had studied, the pelvis presented a predominant form, which, on that account alone, became characteristic. He regarded the inlet as being generally oval and of large transverse diameter in the White. * * * Cuneiform and of large antero-posterior diameter in negroes. * * * M. Verneau confirms the assertions of the greater number of his predecessors, as to the reality of the characters of race to be found in the pelvis. Amongst these characters, there are some which have been pointed out in the negro as *indications of animalism.* * * * In fact the verticality of the ilia, and the increase of the antero-posterior diameter of the pelvis in the Negro, have been chiefly insisted upon as recalling characters which may be observed in mammalia generally, and particularly in apes." (*The Human Species*, pp. 397, 398.)

Winchell says, "The Negro pelvis averages but 26 1/2 inches in circumference; that of the White race is 33 inches. In the Negro it is more inclined, which is another quadrumanous

WHAT IS A NIGGER

character. It is also more narrow and elonated." (*Preadamites*, p. 249.) In the greater length and slenderness of the pelvis, the Negro presents another character of the ape.

Topinard gives the relative length of the femur to the tibia as 67.22 in the Negro and 69.73 in the White. (*Anthropology.*)

The highly developed calves of the White, find their strongest contrast in the thin calves of the Negro. This slenderness of the Negroe's calves is another character of the ape. The calves of the White, situated low on the leg, find their strongest contrast in the calves of the Negro, set relatively high on the leg. The elevated position which the calves of the Negro occupy in the leg, is another character of the ape.

The short, narrow heel of the White, finds its strongest contrast in the long, flat foot of the Negro. The latter is another character of the ape.

Topinard in contrasting the following characters of the Negro with those of the White, says: "The femur is less oblique, the tibia more curved, the calf of the leg high and but little

THE CASE OF CENTURIES

developed, the heel broad and projecting, the foot long, but slightly arched, flat, and the great toe rather shorter than in the White. Negresses age rapidly, their breasts elongate after the first preganancy, and become flabby and pendulous." (*Anthropology*, p. 490.)

In discussing the differences presented by the muscles, viscera, vessels, and nerves of the so-called "races of men." Topinard says, "Their study, equally with that of the bones, forms part of the comparative anatomy of man. * * * 'The anatomy in ordinary use with physicians has been acquired in our dissecting rooms, on white subjects, of which there is always a plentiful supply. Some few Negroes and Mongolians have also been submitted to dissection, but without much attention being paid to the subject. It is only now that this branch of anthropology is beginning to spring into life. We begin to find that there are as many reasons why we should search into the differences which exist in internal organs as into the features of the countenance. Some splendid works on the anatomy of foreign

WHAT IS A NIGGER

races have already appeared; anatomical variations, supposed anomolies, are no longer passed by as matters of no interest. * * * 'One fact has been already ascertained-namely, that the muscular system is the seat of differences: some as to the nature of the characters which we have termed unimportant; others produced by arrangements which are found normally in various classes of the Mammalia. The variations exhibited by the cutaneous muscle, the muscles of the face or of the ears, the adductors of the arm, the rectus abdominus muscle, the muscle of the hand and foot, the glutaei, and the triceps of the calf of the leg are in this category. * * * 'All the internal parts of the body are subject to variety in different races: the peritoneum, the ilso-coecal appendix, the liver, the larynx; and if the small number of cases observed did not lead us to fear pronouncing as an individual variation one of an ethnic character, we might mention many examples of them. No doubt special peculiarities in the internal generative organs will be discovered. The nervous system has

THE CASE OF THE CENTURIES

been the subject of closer study. Soemmering, and after him Jacquart, demonstrated that the nerves of the Negro, particularly those of the base of the brain, are larger than those of the European. It has been ascertained that his cerebral substance is not so white. (*Anthropology*, pp. 307, 308, 309.)

Quatrefages says: "Relatively to the white, the Negro presents a marked predominance of peripheral nervous expansians. The truneks are thicker, and the fibres more numerous, or perhaps merely easier to isolate and to preserve on account of their volums alone. On the other hand, the cerebral centres, or at least the brain appear to be inferior in development. " (*The Human Species*, p. 401.)
"There are also some slight variations between the respiration, circulation, animal temperature secretions, etc., of the White man and the Negro; the muscular energy and the manner in which it is employed, sometimes vary considerably in different races; general sensibility, and consequently aptitude for feeling pain, are very

WHAT IS A NIGGER

unequally developed." (*Ibid*, p. 409.)

Dr. Mosely quoted by Winchell says, Negroes are void of sensibility to a surprising degree. They are not subject to nervous diseases. They sleep soundly in every disease, nor does any mental disturbance keep them awake. They bear chirurgical operations much better than white people; and what would be the cause of insupportable pain to a white man, a negro would almost disregard." (*Preadimites*, p. 178.)

Dr. J. Hendree, of Aniston, Alabama, writing to Dr. Winchell says; "Let me mention one fact especially, drawn from my own experience of forty years. The coarseness of their (the negroes) organization makes them require about double the dose of ordinary medicine used for the whites." Dr. M. L. Barrow, of Drayton, Georgia, writing to Dr. Winchell say: "I have practiced among the negroes over forty years * * * Your information in respect to the doses of medicine for the colored people corresponds with my experience-except as regards opiates; and perhaps they will bear large

THE CASE OF THE CENTURIES

quantities of these, as I have known some to take very large doses with impunity," (*Ibid*, p. 177.)

The highly developed pilious system of the white, finds its strongest contrast in the deficient pilious system of the negro. Of the latter Topinard says' "The beard is scant and developed late. The body is destitute of hair, except on the pubis and armpits." (*Anthropology*, p. 488.) Winchell says, "As to the pilious system it is deficient in the Negro. The hairs of the head are black and crispy, with a tranverse section, and are inserted vertically in the scalp. The skin is black, velvety and comparatively cool. (*Ibid*, p. 174.)

"In the Negro, the development of the body is generally in advance of the white. His wisdom teeth are cut sooner; and in estimating the age of his skull, we must reckeon it as at least five years in advance of the white." (*Ibid*, p. 175.) "The temperament of the Negro is more sluggish than that of the White man." In Africa, the Negroes are extremely indolent, and use little exertion for their well-being. Every person who

WHAT IS A NIGGER

has resided in the midst of a Negro population in our Southern States has been compelled to remark their incapability of intense effort, and their constitutional sleepiness and slowness. This inability to make great exertions secures them from fatigue, and diminishes the demand for regular periods for total repose and invigorating sleep. "In a true sense, they are in a state of partial sleep during the day, and hence are able to pass night after night without a total suspension of their usual activity." (*Ibid*, pp. 175, 176.)

The person of the White exhales an odor which is scarely perceptable, and not especially offensive. In striking contrast to this, the Negro is characterized by a very stong offensive odor. Topinard says, "The characteristic effuvium from the hold of a slave-ship can never be got rid of." -(*Ibid*.)

Dr. Winchell says, "The exemption of the Negro from malarial diseases, and sundry other pathological affections of the White race is another significant diagnostic. "If the population of New England, Germany, France, England, or

THE CASE OF THE CENTURIES

other northern climates, should come to Mobile, "or to New Orleans, a large proportion die of yellow fever, and if one hundred such individuals landed in the latter city, at the commencement of an epidemic of yellow fever, probably half would fall victims to it. On the contrary, Negroes, under all circumstances, enjoy an almost perfect exemption from this disease, even though brought in from our nothern states."-*Preadimites*, p. 180.) Quatreages says, "Of all human races the White is the most sensitive to marsh fevers, and the Black the least so. On the other hand the Negro race suffers more than any other from phthisis." -(*The Human Species*, p. 426.)

Dr. Winchell says, "The mental indolence of Negroes is further shown in the comparative records of insanity and idiocy. While among Whites, mania occurs in the proportion of 0.76 per thousand, among Negroes it is only 0.10 per thousand. While idiocy, among the former, is 0.73 per thousand, among the latter it is 0.37 per thousand." -*Preadimites*, p. 182.)

Dr. Winchell quotes Mr. William Morrow,

WHAT IS A NIGGER

Chesterville, Ohio, (The Transcript, published by the students of the Ohio Wesleyan University, Delaware, Ohio, Oct. 1878), who says:

"In early life I had conceived a horror of slavery in all its forms, and had long held to the opinion that the Negro, once free, and having a fair opportunity, would surely make rapid progress toward becoming a good and honorable citizen. I expected a good deal more than I have found." "After narrating the extent and variety of his experiences in New Orleans, Huntsville [Alabama], and Nashville, he gives his conclusions lead as follows:" "As a rule, the Negro does not learn as well as do children of this state [Ohio]. Some things they seem to master readily; but when they come to any reasoning they usually fail. They read well if they have a good teacher, and nearly all write well. In arithmetic, grammer, geography and the higher branches, they are mostly deficient. They learn definitions tolerable well, but fail in the application. In arithmetic, a class may learn a method of solving examples, and will work them

THE CASE OF THE CENTURIES

with wonderful facility. You pass on a week or so with the class, come to a place requiring the use of the principle formerly learned, and it is gone. I had in my charge a class in arithmetic that had been half way through the book; upon examination, I found that not a single one of them could work an example in long division. * * * Some of those who are teaching, of course, are more intellgent, many being able to teach arithmetic as far as decimals and interest. I meet very few who know anything about grammar. * * * 'Fear is usually the only thing that controls them. Very few of the finer feelings find any lodgement in their natures. Having been once taught to obey, they do moderately well. The coarse nature is easily aroused, and they have never heard tell of such a thing as self-control. Their anger knows no bounds, often attacking a teacher in open school * * * A Negro knows no bashfulness; no feeling of diffidence in the presence of superior ever troubles him. If accused of anything, they assume a look of injured innocence that would credit the veriest saint in

WHAT IS A NIGGER

the calendar. They never plead guilty, and have an excuse for any and all occurrences." -[*Ibid*, pp. 183,184.]

The doctrine was once universally taught, and is still entertained by many that, the dark complexion of the Negro, and that of the other so-called "colored races of men" is due to climatic influence. Scientific research has long since demonstrated the fallacy of this absurd hypothesis. In discussing this subject, Dr. Winchell says:

"The yellow-tawny Hottentots live side by side with the black Kaffirs. The ancient Indians of California, in the latitude of 42 degrees, were as black as the Negroes of Guinea, while in Mexico were tribes of an olive or reddish complexion, relatively light. So in Africa, the darkest Negroes are 12 or 15 degree north latitude; while their color becomes lighter the nearer they approach the equator." "The Yoloffs," says Goldberry, "are a proof that the black color does not depend entirely on solar heat, nor on the fact that they are more exposed

THE CASE OF THE CENTURIES

to a vertical sun, but arises from other causes; for the further we go from the influence of its rays, the more the black color is increased in intensity," So we may contrast the dark-skinned Eskimo with the fair Kelts of temperate Europe. If it be thought that extreme cold exerts upon color an influence similar to that of extreme heat, we may compare the dark Eskimo with the fair Finns of similar latitudes. Among the black races of tropical regions we find generally some light colored tribes interspersed. These sometimes have light hair and blue eyes. This is the case with the Tuareg of the Sahara, the Affghans of India, and the aborigines of the banks of the Orinoco and the Amazon. The Abyssinians of the plains are lighter colored than those of the heights; and upon the low plains of Peru, the Antisians are of fairer complexion than the aymaras and Quichuas of the high table-lands. Humboldt says: "The Indians of the Torrid Zone, who inhabit the most elevated plains of the Cordillera of the Andes, and those who are engaged in fishing at the 45th degree of south

WHAT IS A NIGGER

latitude, in the islands of the Chonos Archipelago, have the same copper color as those who, under a scorching climate, cultivate the banana in the deepest and narrowest valleys of the Equinoctial region." (*Ibid*, pp. 185, 186. See also Topinard's *Anthropology*, pp. 386, 387.)

In explaining the real cause of the differences in *Complexion*, which we observe among the so-called "races of men, Topinard says:

"The color of the skin, hair and eyes is the result of a general phenomenon in the organism, namely, the production and distribution of the coloring matter. The skin of the Scandinavian is white, almost without color, or rather rosy and florid, owing to the transparency of the epidermis allowing the red coloring matter of the blood to be sun circulating through the capillaries. * * * "The skin of the Negro of Guinea, and especially of Yoloff, the darkest of all, is, on the contrary, jet black, which is caused by the presence in the minute cellules on the deep surface of the epidermis of black granulus, known by the name

THE CASE OF THE CENTURIES

of pigment. The black layer thus formed by these cellules, which used to be called *rete mucosum* of Malpighi, remains adherent sometimes to the dermis and sometimes to the epidermis on removing the latter, after previously submitting the skin to maceration. This pigment is found in all races, whether black, yellow or white, but in very different quantity; hence their various tones of color, from the lightest to the darkest whites, who readily become brown on exposure to light, are undoubtedly provided with it. It is always more abundant in the scrotum and round the nipple. It is very visible on the mucous membrane of negroes, which are frequently surrounded by masses of it, notably on the vault of the palate, the gums, and the conjunctiva, which we have also met with in young orangs. (*Anthropology*, pp. 342, 343.)

In discussing this subject Quatrefages says "With all anthropologists I recognize the high value of the color of the skin as a character. * * * We know that it does not result from the exitence or disappearance of special layers. Black

WHAT IS A NIGGER

or White, the skin always comprises a white *dermis*, penetrated by many capillaries, and *epidemis*, more or less transparent and colorless. Between the two is placed the *mucous layer*, of which the *pigment* alone in reality varies in quantity and color according to the race. All the colors presented by the human skin have two common elements, the white of the dermis and the red of the blood. Moreover, each has its own proper element, resulting from the colorings of the pigment. The rays reflected from these different tissues combine into a resultant which produces the different tints and traverses the epidermis. The latter plays the part of roughened glass. The more delicate and the finer it is, the more perceptible is the color of the subjacent parts. * * * From the preceding, we can also understand why the White alone can be said to turn pale or to blush. The reason is, that in him the pigment allows the slighest differences in the afflux of blood to the dermis to be perceived. With the Negro as with us, the blood has its share in the coloring, the tint of which it deepens or

THE CASE OF THE CENTURIES

modifies. When the blood is wanting, the Negro turns gray from the blending of the white of the dermis with the black of the pigment." (*The Human Species*, pp. 356, 357.)

Thus, it is shown by the highest scientific authorities, that the black, colorless complexion of the Negro, is not the result of climatic influence; but it is due solely to the black pigment, which intervenes between the dermis and the epidermis. This pigment, like every other part of the organism, is subject to disease. One of the disease to which the pigment is liable is known as albinism. The victims of this disease are termed albinos. In discusing albinism, and albinos, Dr. Topinard says:

"Albinos are individuals in whom the pigmentary matter is so far deficient that the skin and hair are colorless, the iris is transparent, and the choriod coat destitute of the dark pigment for the absorption of redundant rays of light. In consequence of this, they are unable to bear sunlight, and see better at night than during the day. Their eyeballs are affected with a perpetual

WHAT IS A NIGGER

oscillating movement, their skin and hair are colorless, or of a dull white, the eyes reddish, the transparency of the tissues showing the blood circulating through the capillaries. They are often indolent, and without muscular vigor. There are partial aibinos, in whom the above symptoms are observed, but in a less degree. They easily pass unnoticed among the white races, but are very observable among the black; their eyes are light blue or reddish. Both are met with among all races and under all climates. In some of the native courts on the west coast of Africa, especially in Congo, they are an object of verneration, and go by the name of 'dondos.' Dr. Schweinfurth has seen a great number of them with the King of the Menbouttous on the banks of the Bahr-el-Ghazel. From their presence among the blackest populations, Prichard framed an important argument in favor of the influence of external circumstances, and of the derivation of the human race from one primitive pair. He delighted to reiteate it, and, moreover, he was the first to establish the fact that their hair was as

THE CASE OF THE CENTURIES

wooly, and their features were as negro as their fellow countrymen of the same tribe. We say again, albinism is only a monstrosity, a pathological condition which has been cured, and we must take care how we place implicit reliance on the confused accounts given of it by travellers." (*Anthropology*, p. 161.)

Scientific research has also demonstrated that the differences which we observe in the form and texture of the hair, among the so-called "races of men," is not the result of climatic influence. Dr. Winchell says:

"The condition of the hair is found to sustain relations to climate no more exact than the complexion. The Tasmanians, in latitude forty-five degrees, had hair as wooly as that of the Negroes under the equator. On the contrary, smooth hair is found extensively in tropical latitudes, as among the Australians, the Blacks of the Deccan (India), and the Himejarites of the Yemen, in Arabia. * * * Similar absence of correlation between stature and the environment has been ascertained." [*Preadimites*, pp. 186,

WHAT IS A NIGGER

187.]

Dr. Topinard says, "No explanation can be given as to the varieties of the hair in its fundamental types. For example, the straight and the round, the wooly and flat hair, as seen under the microscope. In this lies the most serious objection to the theory of the derivation of characters from one another. In the resent state of science we have no explanation to give on the subject." -(*Anthropology*, pp. 391, 392.)

The utterance of this eminent anthropologist should receive our most serious consideration. With his occustomed candor, he frankly admits that science can give no explanation as to why the hair of the white is long, smooth, fine and round, and is inserted obliquely in the scalp; while in striking contrast to these characters, the hair of the Negro, is short, coarse, wooly, and flat; and is inserted vertically in the scalp. [2] He calls attention to the fact that, in these opposite characters, "lies the most serious objection to the theory of the derivation of characters from one another," or,

THE CASE OF THE CENTURIES

in other words in these opposing characters, lies the most serious onjection to the theory that either the Negro or the White, is the result of development, the one from the other; and also presents the most serious objection to the theory that the White and the Negro, are the descendants of one primitive pair.

Thus it is shown by comparative anatomy that the Negro, from the crown of his wooly head, to the sole of his flat foot, differs in his physical and mental organisms from the White; and that "just in proportion as he differs from the White, he approximates the lower animals."

WHAT IS A NIGGER

Chapter IV.
Convincing Biblical and Scientific Evidence that the Negro is not of the Human Family.

The following measurements of brain weights collected by Sanford B. Hunt, in the Federal army during the late war in the United States, demonstrated that the White blood is the lever which elevates; and that the Negro blood is the lever which lowers the mental grade of individuals, tribes, nations, continents, and the world at large.

      Weight of brain
      Grammes.
"24 Whites..................................1424
25 Three parts white....................1390
47 Half-white, or mulattoes..........1334
51 One-quarter white...................1319
95 One-eighth white.....................1308
22 A sixteenth white 1280
141 Pure negroes..........................1331"
[*Topinard's Anthropology*, p. 312.]

THE CASE OF THE CENTURIES

These estimates are accepted by the scientific world, are quoted by Topinard, Quatrefages, Winchell, and others. Though these measurements are fair to the Negro, and to the classes of mixed bloods to which they refer, they are obviously unfair to the pure Whites, for the following reasons: (1) They were evidently taken from the common soldiers of the Federal army; the higher grades of army officers and the more intelligent classes in the various peaceful vocations in the United States were not represented. Had they been, the average brain weight of the Whites would have been raised to the average of the Noachites-1500 grammes.
(2) More or less of the soldiers whom Dr. Hunt recognized as pure whites may have had some admixture of negro blood; and this, as shown by his table, would have reduced the brain weight of such individuals; and would, of course, have reduces the average to this extent. Hence, in the present amalgamated condition of the world, it is evident that it would be unjust to take the average

WHAT IS A NIGGER

of brain weights in almost any assemblage of individuals, or in any nation, or continent, as representing that of the pure whites.

Topinard, in discussing Hunt's measurements, says, "This would lead us to believe that the mixed breeds assimilate the bad more readily than the good."
(*Ibid*, p. 312.)

These measurements are invaluable in that they prove that man is a distinct creation. They also demonstrate that the whites and the negroes are not different races of the same species. One of the great difficulties which breeders experience in their attempt to produce new varieties by crossing is the strong disposition of the offspring to resort to one or the other of its parent stocks. But not so with the offspring of whites and negroes. As has been shown, the offspring of man and the negro, if bred continuously to pure whites for ages, could never become pure white; you could never breed the ape out, nor breed the spiritual creation in. Hence, they would remain simply mixed bloods, without

THE CASE OF THE CENTURIES

reference to what their physical and mental characters might be. These measurements demonstrate that if the offspring of whites and negroes were bred continuously to negroes for ages they would never become negroes, but would remain mixed bloods.

If whites and negroes were different races of the same species, their immediate offspring should take a position, on point of brain weight, midway between the two; thus presenting a brain weight of at least 1377 1/2 grammes. But, instead of this, the half-whites present an average of 1334 grammes, only three grammes in excess of the Negro, and 90 grammes less than that of the common white soldier of the Federal army. Then mate the half-white with pure negroes and you would reduce the white blood from one-half to one-quarter, and increase the negro blood from one-half to three quarters; and the off spring presents a brain weight of 1319 grammes, which is 12 grammes less than that of the pure negro. Then mate the one-quarter white with pure negroes and you reduce the white blood in their

WHAT IS A NIGGER

offspring from one-quarte to one-eighth, and increase the negro blood from three-quarters to seven-eighths; and the offspring presents a brain weight 1308 grammes, which is 23 grammes less than that of the pure negro. Then mate the one-eighth white with pure negroes, and you reduce the white blood in the offspring from one-eighth to one-sixteenth, and increase the negro blood from seven-eighths to fifteen-sixteenths, and the offspring presents a brain weight of only 1280 grammes, which is 51 grammes less than that of the pure negro.

This is as far as Dr. Hunt's measurements extended. But, it is evident that, with this rapid fall of brain weight in each succeeding generation, if the process were continued, their offspring would finally descend in point of brain weight to the level of the gorilla, whose brain weight is placed by Huxley at 600 grammes.

When we compare the brain weight of whites with that of "the Hottentot, 974," and with that of "the Australian, 907 grammes," we find that, as Winchell says, "The significance of

THE CASE OF THE CENTURIES

these comparisons appears when we learn that Broca, the most eminent of French anthropolgists, states that when the European brain falls below 978 grammes [mean of males and females], the results is idiocy. In this opinion Thurman coincides." [*Preademites*, pp. 249. 259] Dr. Schaaffhausen, quoted by Huxley, says the brain weight of "the diminutive Hindoos falls to as little as 27 ounces." [*Man's Place in Nature*, p. 160.]

These diminutive brain weights, carrying with them a corresponding dimunition of intelligence, would, in a civilized community, place the individuals in the lowest grades of society; at the same time they might never suffer for the want of food. Hence, their physical development might not be impaired. But, if driven into the forest and compelled to battle with adverse conditions, of climate, etc., they would suffer long periods of want, and this repeated at frequent intervals for many centuries would necessarily impair their physical development; and finally their physical

WHAT IS A NIGGER

organisms would become as degraded as their mental. Thus, it becomes evident that the mixed bloods in whom the blood of the Negro largely predominates over that of the Whites, are more degraded and ape-like in their physical and mental organisms; and consequently are more depraved in their modes of life, customs, habits, language, manners, gestures, etc., than the pure Negro. This alone can explain the following facts cited by Winchell, who says:

"The measurements already given show the Australians to possess an organism quite inferior to that of the Negro. In intelligence he is said to be so low as to be unable to count over four or five. Of the Aetas of the Phillippines, De la Geronniere says that they gave him the impression of being a great tribe of monkeys; their voices recalled the short cry of these animals, and their movements strengthened the analogy. Buchner says that the toes of these savages, who live partly in grottoes, partly on trees, are 'very mobile,' and more separated than ours, especially the great toe. They use them in

THE CASE OF CENTURIES

maintaining themselves on branchs and cords, as with fingers. According to Buchner, 'the language of the savages of Borneo is rather a kind of warbling, or croaking, than a truly human mode of expression.' 'The Veddahs of Ceylon,' says Sir Emerson Tennant, 'communicate among themselves almost entirely by means of signs, grimaces, gutteral sounds, resembling very little true words, or true language.' 'The Dokes of Abyssinia,' according to Krapt, 'are human pigmies; they are not more than four feet high; their skin is of an olive brown. Wanderers in the woods, they live like animals, without habitations, without sacred trees, etc. They go naked, nourishing themselves by roots, fruit, mice, serpents, ants, honey; they climb trees like monkeys. Without chief, without law, without arms, without marriage, they have no family, and mate by chance like animals; they also multiply rapidly. The mother after a short lactation, abandons her child to itself. They neither hunt nor cultivate, nor sow, and have never known the use of fire. They have thick

WHAT IS A NIGGER

lips, a flattened nose, little eyes, long hair, hands and feet with great nails, with which they dig the soil.' Some of the American tribes remain at the lowest point of degradation. This is the case with the Fuegians, and the Botecudos of Brazil have often been cited. Of the latter Lallimand says, 'I am sadly convinced that they are monkeys with two hands.'" [*Preademites*, pp. 267, 268.]

The following is Cuvier's description of the "Hottentot Venus," a female Bojesman, "who dies in Paris on the 29th of December, 1815:" "She had a way of pouting her lips exactly like that we have observed in the Orang-Outang. Her movements had something abrupt and fantastical about them, reminding one of those of the ape. Her lips were monstrously large; her ear was like that of many apes, being small, the tragus weak and the external border almost obliterated behind. These are animal characters. Again, I have never seen a human head more like an ape than that of this woman." Referring to the "fatty proturberances" of the haunches, he says: "They offer a striking resemblance to those which exists

THE CASE OF THE CENTURIES

in the females of the mandritts, the papions, etc., and which assume, at certain epochs of their life, an enlargement truly monstrous."

"In the dissection of a Bojesman by M. L. Testut [Acad. des. Sci., Paris, 7 July, 1884; Science, xxx., 284] a muscular system in a more or less rudimentary state was revealed-such as exists in a normal condition, in various anthropoid and other apes, and in some instances even in the mammals of other orders." [*Preademities.*]

These facts taken in connection with Hunt's measurement of brain weights, showing the effects of amalgamation on cerebral development, fully confirm the following conclusions. (1) When whites and negroes are mated the brain weight of their offspring is neither that of the white nor that of the negro; the same is true of his physical characters, he is neither white nor black, but colored. You would thus produce a new, so-called race of men, with an average brain weight of 1,334 grammes. Let us suppose that there are 1,500 of these half-breeds, and that 500 of them find mates among

WHAT IS A NIGGER

themselves; their offspring would be half-breeds with a brain weight of 1,334 grammes. Then suppose that we mate another 500 of the half-breeds with pure whites, this offspring would be three-quarter white; and would present a brain weight of 1,390 grammes. You would thus produce another so-called, "race of men." Then suppose we mate the remaining 500 half-breeds with pure negroes, their offspring would be one-quarter white; and would present a brain weight of 1,319 grammes. You would thus produce another "race of men," making in all three new and distinct classes of creatures, as widely different in their physical, as in their mental characters. If each class of these creatures now isolated from the rest of the world and their marriage relations confined to their own class, they would finally settle down to some fixed type. It is easy to say that the number of these so-called "races of men," could be increased almost indefinitely, by mating the mixed bloods with pure whites, with pure negroes, and with mixed bloods of different grades; the progeny of each

THE CASE OF THE CENTURIES

cross would present a new type of man, when viewed from the standpoint of Natural Development. We observe that, between the white Federal soldier and the negro there is a difference in point of brain weight, of 93 grammes; while between the three-quarter white, and the one-sixteenth white, there is a difference in point of brain weight, of 110 grammes. Thus we have a greater difference in point of brain weight, between the extremes of mixed bloods, as shown by Hunt's measurements, that exists between the whites and negroes. Hence, we might lay the whites and negroes aside, and still have a wider range for the production of new "races of men," by crossings among the different grades of mixed bloods; and this range could be largly increased by mating the progeny of the three-quarter whites, with whites; and by mating the progeny of the one-sixteenth white with negroes. In the former the increase of brain weight would correspond with the increased predominance of white blood; while in the latter the decrease in brain weight would correspond

WHAT IS A NIGGER

with the increased predominance of negro blood; and these differences in their mental characters, would be accompanied with corresponding differences in their physical characters. The rapid decrease in brain weight resulting from each infusion of negro blood, as shown by Hunt's measurements, demonstrates that, if the progeny of the one-sixteenth white was mated continously with negroes for generations, they would finally descend as low, or perhaps lower in point of brain weight, than "the diminutive Hindoos" - "27 ounces." There are doubtless other tribes of mixed bloods whose brain weight is even nearer that of the gorilla. The brain weight of many of the lower grades of mixed-blooded tribes have never been ascertained.

(2) They prove that the White and the Negro are not the same kind of flesh, from the fact that the offspring resulting from their unions cannot revert to either of its parent stocks.

(3) They prove the truth of Paul's declaration that " all flesh is not the same flesh; but there is one kind of flesh of men, another

THE CASE OF THE CENTURIES

flesh of beasts," etc.

(4) They prove that the Negro belongs to the flesh of beasts, from the fact that his offspring by man, though mated continuously with negroes will not revert to the Negro, but approximates a lower grade of animal. Further evidence of this is found in the fact that the mixed bloods frequently develop characters which are never found in either the pure white or the pure negro, but which are peculiar to lower grades of animals. From the many which the want of space forbids us to enumerate, we shall select the following:

"A character of the humerus, or arm bone, was remarked by Cuvier, which approximates the Bushmen to monkeys, dogs and other carnivores, as well as to the wild boar, chevrotian and the daman. It was the non-ossification of the wall separating the anterior cubital fossa from the posterior fossa of the humerus-something which will be intelligible to persons versed in anatomy." (*Preadimites.*) Such also is "tablier" and "steatopygia." Of these Topinard says, "Hitherto we have met with many opposite

WHAT IS A NIGGER

characters in the human groups, but few so remarkable as these. We have seen the marked difference between woolly and straight hair, between the prognathous and the orthognathous, the jet black of the Yoloff and the pale complexion of the Scandianavian, between the ultra-dolichocephalic Esquimau or New Caledonian and the ultra-brachycepalic Mongolian. But the line of separation between the European and Bosejesman as regards these two characters is, in a morphological point of view, still wider, as much so as between each of the anthropoid apes, or between the dog and the wolf, the goat and the sheep." (*Anthropology*, p. 363.) The Bushman, or Bosjesman, and the Hottentots are classed by Winchell as one race. Topinard describes the Hottentots as "an agglomeration of ancient races."

These, and other animal characters in the mixed breeds, have been seized upon by the advocates of the Theory of Development as proof that man developed from a lower form; and these animal characters were transmitted from his

THE CASE OF THE CENTURIES

"animal ancestors." The very reverse is true. The creatures possessing these characters are the result of amalgamation between two different kinds of flesh; the flesh of men and the flesh of beasts. The mere fact that these creatures frequently develop characters which are common to the "flesh of beasts," should occasion no surprise when viewed in the light of Paul's declaration as to the different kinds of flesh. The wonder is that they don't develop a tail; and if one or more individuals of these so-called "lower races of men" is found either alive or in a fossil state, with such an appendage, an intelligent examination of his anatomy will reveal the evidences of crossing. Let us bear in mind that the negro, the lower apes and the quadrupeds, all belong to "one kind of flesh," the "flesh of beasts." Hence it should rather be surprising, than otherwise, if the Negro did not transmit to the offspring resulting from his unnatural union with man, characters which are not only common to the lower apes, but even those which are common to quadrupeds. The mixed-bloods are

WHAT IS A NIGGER

"an unnatural production," and being altogether "out of the common order of nature," they are simply monstrosities, no odds what their social, political, or religious standing may be. Even the atheist, who denies the existence of a God and the inspiration of the scriptures, will insist that amalgamation between Whites and Negroes is "a violation of the natural law." For thousands of years these base-born creatures have been found in every position in life, from the jungle to the throne. In thousands of cases they live sumptuously, and are arrayed in "purple and fine linen," and bedecked with jewels and all the paraphenalia of their inherited wealth and rank. In other cases, like that of many of our newly acquired "brothers and sisters of the Phillipines," they obtain a bare subsistence from the spontaneous products of the earth, and the proceeds of the chase, and are simply attired "in atmosphere and smiles."

For further evidence of the frequent appearance of "animal characters" in the so-called "lower races of men," see the works of

THE CASE OF THE CENTURIES

Cuvier, Winchell, Darwin, Huxley, Haeckel, etc.

The existence of a tool-making animal should occasion us no surprise, when we consider the fact that lower grades of ape than the Negro handle tools for a particular purpose. Mr. Darwin says,

"It has often been said that no animal uses any tool, but the chimpanzee in a state of nature cracks a native fruit, somewhat like a walnut, with a stone. Renger easily taught an American monkey thus to break open hard palmnuts, and afterward of its own accord it used stones to open other kinds of nuts, as well as boxes. It thus also removed the soft rind of fruit that had a disagreeable flavor. Another monkey was taught to open the lid of a large box with a stick, and afterward it used the stick as a lever to move heavy bodies; and I have myself seen a young ourang put a stick into a crevice, slip his hand to the other end, and use it in the proper manner as a lever.

* * * In these several cases, stones and sticks were employed as implements; but they are

WHAT IS A NIGGER

likewise used as weapons. Brehm states, on the authority of the well-known traveler, Schimper, that in Abyssinia when the baboons belonging to one species (C. gelada) descend in troops from the mountains to plunder the fields they sometimes encounter troops of another species (C. hamadoyas), and then a fight ensues. The Geledas roll down great stones, which the Hamadoyas try to avoid, and then both species, making a great uproar, rush furiously against each other. Brehm, when accompanying the Duke of Coburg-Gotha, aided in an attack with firearms on a troop of baboons in the pass of Mensa in Abyssinia. The baboons in return rolled so many stones down the mountains, some as large as a man's head, that the attackers had to beat a hasty retreat, and the pass was actually closed for a time against the caravan. It deserves notice that these baboons thus acted in concert." (*Descent of Man*, pp. 91,92.)

Mr. Hartman says, "Buffon's Chimpanze offered people his arm, walked with them in orderly manner, sat down to table like a man,

THE CASE OF THE CENTURIES

opened his napkin and wiped his lips with it, made use of his spoon and fork, poured out wine and clinked glasses, fetched a cup and saucer and put in sugar, poured out tea, let it get cold before drinking it. * * * He ate all the ordinary food of men, but preferred fruit. * * * He was friendly with every one, coming close to them, and taking pleasure in their caresses. He took such a fancy to one lady, that when other people approached her he seized a stick and began flourishing it about, until Buffon intimated his displeasures at such conduct." (*Anthropoid Apes*, p. 267.)

According to the account of Captain Grandpre, a female chimpanzee on board his vessel would heat the oven, taking care that no coals fell out, and carefully watching until it was of the right heat, of which she would inform the baker. She fulfilled all the duties of a sailor, such as drawing up the anchor, furling and making fast the sails. She patiently endured maltreatment by a brutal mate, stretching out her hands imploringly to ward off the blows. But after this

WHAT IS A NIGGER

she refuse all food, and died in five days of grief and hunger." (*Ibid*, p. 268.)

Mr. Darwin says, "Monkeys seize thin branches or ropes, with the thumb on one side and the fingers and palm on the other, in the same manner as we do. * * * They seize nuts, insects, or other small objects with the thumb in opposition to the fingers. * * * Monkeys open mussel shells with two thumbs. * * * With their fingers they pull out thorns and burrs, and hunt for each other's parasites. They roll down stones, or throw them at their enemies; nevertheless, they are clumsy in these various actions, and, as I have myself seen, are quite unable to throw a stone with precision." (*Ibid*, pp. 56, 57.)

"A male chimpanzee, which was kept in the Berlin Aquarium in 1876 * * * was on particularly friendly terms with Dr. Hermes' two-year-old-boy. When the child entered the room, the chimpanzee ran to meet him, embraced and kissed him, seized his hands and drew him to

THE CASE OF THE CENTURIES

the sofa, that they might play together. The child was often rough with his playfellow, pulling him by the mouth, pinching his ears, or lying on him, yet the chimpanzee was never known to lose his temper. He behaved very differently to boys from six to twelve years old. When a number of school-boys visited the office, he ran towards them, went from one to the other, shook one of them, bit the leg of another, seized the jacket of a third with the right hand, jumped up, and with the left gave him a sound box on the ear; in short he played the wildest pranks. * * * One day when Hermes gave his nine-year-old son a slight rap on the head, on account of some miscalculation in his arithmetic, the chimpanzee, who was also sitting at the table, gave the boy a smart box on the ear. * * * When he saw that Hermes was writing, he often seized a pen, dipped it in the inkstand, and scrawled upon the paper. He displayed a special talent for cleaning the window-panes of the aquarium. It was amusing to see him squeezing up the cloth, moistening the pane with his lips, and then rubbing it hard,

WHAT IS A NIGGER

passing quickly from one place to another." (*Anthropoid Apes*, pp. 270, 271.) "An ourang brought by Montgomery to Calutta in 1827 * * * tried to scour his tin vessel with a cloth, throwing one end over his shoulder, as he had seen the servants of the house do." (*Ibid*, p. 279.)

Mr. Hartman says, "Mafuca was a remarkable creature, not only in her external habits, but in her disposition. At one moment she would sit still with a brooding air, only occasionally darting a mischievous, flashing glance at the spectators, at another she took pleasure in feats of strength, or she seemed to roam to and fro in her spacious enclosure like an angry beast of prey. She would insert the index finger of her right hand in the opening of a vessel that weighed thirty pounds, climb up the pole with it, and let it fall with a crash and clatter from a height of six feet.
* * * She hardly obeyed any one except Mr. Schopf, the director of the Dresden Zoological Gardens, and when in a good humor she would sit on his knee and put her muscular arms around

THE CASE OF THE CENTURIES

his neck with a caressing gesture. In spite of this, Schopf was never secure from Mafuca's roguish tricks, since her good humor was of short duration. She was rather fond of the keeper, but not always obedient to him.
* * * Mafuca was able to use a spoon, although somewhat awkwardly, and she could pour from larger vessels into smaller ones without spilling the liquor. She took tea and cocoa in the morning and evening, and a mixed diet between whiles, such as fruit, sweetmeats, red wine and water, and sugar.   * * * If she was left alone for any time, she tried to open the lock of her cage without having the key, and she once succeeded in doing so. On that occasion she stole the key, which was hanging on the wall, hid it in her axilla, and crept quietly back to the cage. With the key she easily opened the lock, and she also knew how to use a gimlet. She would draw off her keeper's boots, scramble up to some place out of reach with them and throw them at his head when he asked for them. She could wring out a wet cloth and blow her nose with a

WHAT IS A NIGGER

handerkerchief.

* * * Just before her death from consumption, she put her arms around Schopf's neck when he came to visit her, looked at him placidly, kissed him three times, stretched out her hand to him and died. The last moments of anthropoids have their tragic side!" (*Ibid*, pp.271, 72, 73.)

Mr. Darwin says, "Sir Andrew Smith, a zoologist whose scrupulous accuracy was known to many persons, told me the following story, of which he himself was an eye-witness: At the Cape of Good Hope an officer had often plagued a certain baboon, and the animal, seeing him approach on Sunday for parade, poured water into a hole and hastily made some thick mud which he skillfully dashed over the officer as he passed by, to the amusement of many bystanders. For a long time afterward the baboon rejoiced and triumphed whenever he saw his victim." (*Ibid*, p. 78.)

Mr. Darwin says, "Mr Wallace on three occasions saw female ourangs, accompanied by their young, breaking off branches and the great,

THE CASE OF THE CENTURIES

spicey fruit of the Durian tree with every appearance of rage, causing such a shower of missiles as effectually kept us from approaching too near the tree." As I have repeatedly seen, a chimpanzee will throw any object at hand at a person who offends him; and the before-mentioned baboon at the Cape of Good Hope prepared mud for the purpose. In the zoological gardens a monkey, which had weak teeth, used to break open nuts with a stone; and I was assured by the keepers that after using the stone he hid it in the straw and would not let any other monkey touch it." (*Ibid*, p. 92.)

Mr. Topinard says: "Many species of monkeys, like Man, select a chief, who directs their operations and to whom they submit. The howlers, or mycites, belonging to the Cebin family, hold meetings in which one of them speaks for hours at a time in the midst of a general silence, succeeded by great excitement, which ceases as soon as the speaker gives the word of command. Other monkeys combine together to plan an excursion; divided into

WHAT IS A NIGGER

detachments, some plunder and tear up roots, others make a chain for the purpose of carrying them from hand to hand; others are placed as sentinels to keep watch. In unexpected danger, the sentinels gives the alarm and all decamp. It has been remarked that if the troop is surprised, owing to the fault of the sentinel, there is a grand hub-bub in the neighboring forest during the night, and on the morrow the body of one of the plunderers is found, to all appearance having been put to death by his companions." (*Anthropology*, p. 151.)

These, and many other proofs which might be adduced, enable us to see how closely the lower apes approach the Negro, in their ability to handle tools. Yet we must admit that, the lower apes, and even the so-called anthropoids, are unfit for general domestic purposes. They could never handle domestic animals, work metals, level forests, break the soil, plant, cultivate, and harvest crops, and erect mechanical structures; in short perform the multitudinous duties of servants. Besides, no one of the so-called

THE CASE OF THE CENTURIES

anthropoids, can be said to be "most absolutely like man. The Gorilla approaches nearest to man in the structure of the hand and foot, the Chimpanzee in important structural details in the skull, the Ourang in the development of the brain, and the Gibbon in that of the thorax." (Haeckel, *The Evolution of Man*, p. 181.)

Darwin says, "One can hardly doubt that a man-like animal who possessed a hand and arm sufficiently perfect to throw a stone with precision or to form a flint into a rude tool could, with sufficient practice, as far as mechanical skill alone is concerned, make almost anything which a civilized man can make." (Ibid, p.56.)

The force of Mr. Darwin's reasoning upon this subject is plain. It is easy to see that an animal who could realize his need of a weapon and was possessed of mechanical skill sufficient to enable him to fashion for himself a rudely-chipped weapon of stone, which he could handle with precision, could, if properly trained, make and handle any implement that a man could make and handle. Add to this the fact that the Negro is

WHAT IS A NIGGER

the highest grade of ape and that the disposition of this family of animals to imitate the actions of man are more highly developed in the Negro than in any other ape, and his ability to discharge all the duties of servant, for which God designed him is fully explained. Desor, quoted by Darwin, "has remarked that no animal voluntarily imitates an action performed by man, until, in the ascending scale, we come to monkeys, which are known to be ridiculous mockers." (Ibid, p. 82.)

The great intellectual qualities which the men of this and preceeding ages have displayed, are the result of inheritance from Adam, upon whom they were a Divine bestowal. Hence, they are transmittible. The low order of the Negro's mentality-his lack of inventive skill-is demonstrated by his meager accomplishments in his undomesticated state, which, as has been shown, are confined to the fashioning of a few rude weapons of stone; while the greater achievements of the domesticated Negro are due solely to the influence of man. Hence, if from any cause he is relieved of this influence and is

THE CASE OF THE CENTURIES

thrown upon his own resources in the forest, he soon relapses into savagery and descends to the use of stones for weapons.

Among the older naturalists the opinion prevailed that the apes were quadrumana, or four-handed animals. But this delusion has long since been dispelled. There is no four-handed animal.

But for the existence of the lower apes we, at this late day, would have no alternative than to decide that the Negro is the sole representative of his species or that he is a man. But with this family, shading up from the Lemur to the Negro, we are enabled, with the aids of Scripture and the sciences, to determine that the Negro is a member of it. Thus this interesting family of animals, though unfit for general domestic purposes, are invaluable to man in that they enable him to determine the Negro's proper position in the universe-that he is simply an ape.

But, says the Enlightened Christian, the Negro possesses the moral faculty. Is not this the most positive evidence that he is a man-that

WHAT IS A NIGGER

he has a soul? Not the least evidence! In discussing this question it is essential that we bear in mind that there were just three Creations- Matter, Mind and Soul, and that these made their appearance in the Universe in the order stated. When we accept the teachings of the Bible, we must admit that everything belongs to, and is a part of one or the other of these three creations and necessarily made its appearance in the material universe simultaneously with the Creation of which it is a part. Hence, the question is, which of these three creations is the moral faculty a part of?

Evidently it is not a part of matter, since it does not exist in the plant. Hence, it belongs either to the mind creation, or to the spiritual creation. If it is a part of the latter creation it is peculiar to man. If it is a part of the former creation it is common to man and the animals. It is this faculty-the moral faculty-which enables man to distinguish between right and wrong; and that it is right to obey, and wrong to disobey God. But for the existence of this faculty in man, he could not in justice, be held responsible to God for his acts. This leads us to realize that it is the moral faculty in the animals which makes it possible for man to teach them that it is right to obey, and wrong to disobey their master. But for their possession of this faculty the animals would be unfit for domestic purposes. Hence, inasmuch as the moral faculty does not exist in the plant, in which the matter creation is alone represented, and inasmuch as it is not peculiar to man, in whom the soul creation is alone represented, we have no alternative than to decide that it is a part of the mind creation. Further evidence of this is found in the fact that this faculty, like any physical or mental character, is subject to accident or disease. If from accident or from disease, the mind creation of man, or woman is impaired, the moral faculty is correspondingly impaired. If, as in the case of an insane person, the mind is so impaired as to temporarily, or permanently, destroy the reasoning faculty, the moral faculty is temporarily or permanently destroyed as the case may be. The soul creation of the individual cannot be impaired, and the matter creation as

WHAT IS A NIGGER

presented in the physical structure may not be impaired by its combination with mind that has been injuried or become diseased. The individual may live long after his reasoning faculties have been destoyed. But the very moment he ceases to be a rational being, he ceases to be a moral being. Then, if his mind is restored his moral faculty is restored. The same argument holds good with the animals. The moral, like any faculty of the mind, may be cultivated and developed, or it may be neglected and dwarfed. This can be demonstrated by comparing the cultivated with the uncultivated man; the domesticated with the undomesticated Negro; or our domesticated quadrupeds with the same class of animals in their undomesticated state. When the world of mankind is freed from the thralldom of atheism, and its great intellects are turned upon the Mosaic Record, and the characters peculiar to each of the three Creations are already ascertained (as they will be), our present opinions as to the characters peculiar to man will be very materially modified. Under the influence of The

THE CASE OF THE CENTURIES

Theory of Natural Development, the Negro has been taken into the family of man; the result is, that we have been led to believe that mind, with its intellectual and moral faculties, articulate speech, the erect posture, a well developed hand and foot, the ability to fashion and handle implements are characters peculiar to man. This is a sad mistake. It will yet be ascertained that man has just two characters peculiar to him. (1.) His flesh is a different kind of flesh from that of the lower animals (2.) Man possesses immortality, while the animals are mere creatures of time.

"But, "says the enlightened Christian, "If a man is married to a negress, will not their offspring have a soul?" No; it is simply the product resulting from God's violated law, and inherits none of the Divine nature of the man, but, like its parent, the ape, it is merely a combination of matter and mind. "Then, if the half-breed marries a man, will not their offspring have a soul?" No! "Then if the three-quarter white marries a man will not their offspring have

WHAT IS A NIGGER

a soul?" No. "If the offspring of man and the Negro was mated with pure whites for generations, would not their ultimate offspring have a soul?" No! In discussing this question we must bear in mind that there were just three Creations-matter, mind and soul. That these three creations made their appearance in the order stated. That matter is the basis of all formations in the material universe; whether it exists alone as in the plant, or in combination with mind as in the animal, and with soul as in man. Let us also bear in mind that, the reproduction of these Creations as they exist in the plants, in the animals, and in man, was not left to chance, but is governed by laws which God established in the Creation, and which are unerring and positive in their operations and results.

In order to acquaint ourselves with the operations and results of these laws, let us first discuss the reproduction of plants, in which the matter creation is alone represented; and, since the manner of their reproduction is more generally

THE CASE OF THE CENTURIES

understood, let us take as an illustration, the flowering plants, in which the sexes are represented in the male, and in the female flower. As is well known reproduction results from the union of the pollen, or fecundating dust, of the stamen of the male flower with the pollen of the pistil of the female flower. This indicates that one side or part of the matter creation, exists in the male flower; and that its corresponding side or parts exists in the female flower. These opposite sides are parts, each act as a magnet which attracts its corresponding side or part in the opposite sex; and, when united, the matter creation is perfected and reproduced in the young plant. But, if from any cause, the matter creation, as it exists in its imperfect state in the respective germs of the male and the female flowers, are not united and perfected in the female flower, these vital elements are wasted, and the reproduction of the matter creation in the young plant is not accomplished. The same law holds good with the animal, in which the two Creations-Matter and Mind, exist in the respective germs of the

WHAT IS A NIGGER

male, and the female. One side or part of the Matter Creation, and one side or part of the Mind Creation, exists in an imperfect state in the male germ; the corresponding sides or parts of these imperfect Creations exists in the female germ. By uniting these impefect creations in the female, they are perfected and reproduced in the young animal. This indicates that each of these creations maintains its individuality in their respective male and female germs; and that each side or part of these creations, act as a magnet, which attracts its corresponding side or part in the opposite sex. When sexual union takes place, each side or part of these two creations-Matter and Mind-are united and perfected in the females, conception and birth ensues, and the combination of matter and mind is reproduced in the offspring.

But, if from any cause these imperfect matter and mind creations, as they exist in the respective germs of the male and the female animal, are not united and perfected in the female, these vital elements are wasted, conception does not ensue, and the reproduction of these two

THE CASE OF THE CENTURIES

creations in a young animal is not accomplished. The strength of our position on this subject is demonstrated by the actions of our domestic fowls; it frequently occurs that the female fowl, when not associated with the male fowl, will lay eggs. But only one part of the two creations-matter and mind-as they existed in an imperfect state in the germ of the female were represented in the egg; their corresponding side or part in the male, which was necessary to perfect the creations, was absent. The result of the effort of the female to reproduce these two creations without their corresponding side or part in the male, was abortion-the egg would not "hatch."

The same law holds good with man, in whom the three creations-matter, mind and soul-exist. As in the plant and in the animal, so it must be in man; one side or part of the matter creation, and one side or part of the mind creation, and one side or part of the soul creation exists in the male germ; the corresponding side or part of each of these creations exists in the female germ. Each side or part of these three creations maintains its

WHAT IS A NIGGER

individuality in their respective male and female germs; and each side or part of these three creations acts as a magnet which attracts its corresponding side or part in the opposite sex. When sexual union takes place, each side or part of these three creations unite and are perfected in the female germ; conception ensues and the three creation-matter, mind and soul-are reproduced in the offspring. But when no corresponding side or part of one of these creations exists in the opposite sex, this creation finds no attraction and is passive. Hence, if the sexual act results in conception, this passive creation is not perfected and forms no part of the offspring. For example: In the Negro, as in any other animal, but two creation-matter and mind-are combined. One side or part of each of these creations exists in the male germ; their corresponding side or part exists in the female germ, as mutually dependent sides or parts of the life system of the animal. In the sexual act each of these creations acts as a magnet, which attracts its corresponding side or part in the opposite sex,

THE CASE OF THE CENTURIES

and, if united, these two creations are perfected; conception ensues and the combination of matter and mind is transmitted to the offspring.

Thus, while but two creations-matter and mind-combine to perfect the Negro, three creations-matter, mind and soul-combine to perfect man. While these two creations-matter and mind-exist in an imperfect state in the germs of the male and female Negro, as mutually dependent sides or parts of the life system of the animal, three creations-matter, mind and spiritual life-exist in an imperfect state in the germs of the male and female man, as mutually dependent sides or parts of the life system of man; and such is the attraction between matter and mind as they exist in their imperfect state in the germs of man and the Negro that sexual intercourse between the two will unite and perfect these two creations. But the soul creation in its imperfect and dependent state in the germ of the man, finds no corresponding side or part in the negress. Hence, this creation having no attraction remains passive, and if conception ensues from the union of the

WHAT IS A NIGGER

germs and the consequent perfecting of the matter and mind creations of man and the Negro, this passive creation forms no part of the offspring of this unnatural union. Thus, it is impossible for either side or part of the life system of man-the male or the female-to transmit these three creations-matter, mind and soul to their offspring by the Negro, in whom matter and mind alone exists. In other words, the male and female can only transmit to their offspring such creations as are common to both.

    Let us bear in mind that prior to the creation of man there was no connecting link-no tie of kinship between the Creator and His creatures. All things in the material universe were material, there was nothing spiritual; all was mortal, there was no immortality; but when the Lord God formed man out of "the dust of the ground'" this "dust of the ground" being a part of the original creation-matter- "and breathed into his nostrils the breath of life," spiritual, immortal life, "man became a living soul." This spiritual, immortal life, "this living soul," was a part of the

THE CASE OF THE CENTURIES

substance of God. Hence, its combination with matter and with mind, as presented in man's physical, mental and spiritual organisms, formed the connecting link-the link of kinship-between the Creator and creature. Thus, man became "the Son of God." His failure to form this link of kinship between Himself and the fish, or fowl, or beast, clearly demonstrates the design of God that no kinship should exist between them. Hence, when man becomes so degenerated as to associate himself carnally with the Negro, the very act brings into operation the law which governs the reproduction of the creations, which makes it impossible for man to transmit to his offspring by the beast the slightest vestige of kinship with God.

    This law becomes active and operates with the same result when man associates himself carnally with the mixed breeds; without reference to what their proportions of white and black blood may be. The immediate offspring of man and the Negro-the half breed- like the Negro, is merely a combination of two creations-matter

WHAT IS A NIGGER

and mind. Hence, but two-matter and mind-of the three creatures-matter, mind and soul-as they exist in their imperfect state in the germ of the man find their corresponding sides or portion in the opposite sex of the half breed. The result is, that the one side or part of the soul creation, as it exists in its imperfect state in the germ of the man, finding no corresponding side or part in the opposite sex of the half breed, with which it may be united and perfected, is not attracted and remains passive. Hence, if the matter creation and the mind creation as they exist in their imperfect state in the respective germs of man and the half breed, are united and perfected, and conception ensues, this passive creation forms no part of the offspring. This unvarying law would hold good through millions of generations. Man, in associating himself carnally with the mixed-breeds, would continually oppose three creations-matter, mind and soul-as they exist in their imperfect state in his germ, to only two creations-matter and mind-as they exist in their imperfect state in the germ of the mixed bloods.

THE CASE OF THE CENTURIES

As a result it could only be possible to unite and perfect the matter and mind creations as they exist in their imperfect state in the respective germs of man and the mixed bloods, and thus reproduce and transmit them to the offspring. But the soul creation as it exists in its imperfect state in the germ of man, finding no corresponding side or part in the opposite sex of the mixed bloods with which it might be united and perfected, is not affected in the sexual act and remains passive, hence it is not represented in the offspring.

THE CASE OF THE CENTURIES

Chapter V.
Cain's Offspring Souless, as they were of Amalgamated Flesh.

The atheist takes the negro which God made an ape and thrusts him violently into the family of man as "a lower race of the human species," and enlightened Christianity receives him with open arms; the atheist then points to the remnant of the animals and tells us with much the appearance of truth that there is no beast which with man may associate himself carnally and produce offspring; and enlightened Christianity responds with a hearty Amen! This theory may be good modern philosophy, but it is not scripture, as shown by the following:

"'And Adam knew Eve his wife, and she conceived and bare Cain, and said, I have gotten a man from the Lord. And she again bare his brother Abel. And Abel was a keeper of sheep, but Cain was a tiller of the ground. And in process of time it came to pass that Cain brought

THE CASE OF THE CENTURIES

of the fruit of the ground an offering unto the Lord. And Abel, he also brought of the firstlings of his flock and of the fat thereof. And the Lord had respect unto Abel and to his offerring. But unto Cain and to his offering he had not respect. And Cain was very wroth, and his countenance fell. (Gen.iv, 3-4-5.)"

It will be observed that these brothers were not rivals in business; they were engaged in different pursuits; each offered the products of his labor and skill; and had each of them walked uprightly before God, there could have been no reason why their offerings would not have been alike acceptable to God. But such was not the case. Abel was a good man; he had faith in God (Heb. ii, 4) and respected and obeyed his laws. Hence, "the Lord had respect unto Abel" as a man, and consequently, to his offerings. But Cain was a bad man; the little faith which he had in God, was not expressed in obedience to his laws; he had no respect for the laws of God. Hence, God had no repect for his offering. Cain was a violater of the laws of God, as shown by

WHAT IS A NIGGER

the following:

"'And the Lord said unto Cain, Why art thou wroth, and why is thy countenance fallen? If thou doest well, shalt thou not be accepted? And If thou doest not well, sin lieth at thy door; and unto thee shall be his desire, and thou shalt rule over him.' (Gen. iv, 6-7.)"

This indicates that Cain had not only violated the law of God, but that he had an associate in the crime. To have desire requires life, and also requires intelligence; no inanimate object can have desire. In view of the fact that individuals of the same sex have no desire for each other, it would seem natural to decide that this creature which had desire for this fine young man, Cain, was a female; and the mere fact that the inspired writer refers to it in the masculine gender is no evidence that it was not a female. In describing the animals, it is common in the scriptures to find both sexes referred to in the masculine gender. For example: God made "every winged fowl after his kind.: "'Let the earth bring forth the living creature after his

THE CASE OF THE CENTURIES

kind,'" etc. (Gen. i.: 22-24.)" David refers to the Sun, which is without sex, in the masculine, as follows: "His going forth is from the end of the heave, and his circuit from the ends of it. (Ps. xix, 6.)

We should observe (1) that God charged Cain with sin; (2) that "Unto thee shall be his desire and thou shalt rule over him," was a sentence which God imposed upon Cain and his partner in crime. We should also note the striking similarity of God's language in imposing this sentence to that which he employed in imposing his sentence upon Eve. To the woman who had committed sin, God said, "Thy desire shall be to thy husband, and he shall rule over thee." (Gen. iii, 16.) To the man Cain, who had committed sin, God said, "Unto thee shall be his desire, and thou shalt rule over him." Thus it is shown that the sentence which God imposed upon Eve was identical with that which he imposed upon Cain's partner in sin. In this identity of sentence we find the most positive evidence that Cain's accomplice in the crime which cost him the

WHAT IS A NIGGER

respect of God was a female. In each case God decreed that the desire of the female should be to a particular male, and that the male should "rule over" the female which had desire for him.

In the epistle of Jude we find not only the most positive proof that Cain's partner in sin was a female, but that she was not of Adamic flesh. It will be observed that Jude at once arraigns the men of his day on the charge of amalgamation- "giving themselves over to fornication, and going after strange flesh." And appeals to the followers of the Saviour to "keep" themselves "in the love of God."

Jude says: "Beloved, when I gave all diligence to write unto you of the common salvation, it was needful for me to write unto you and exhort you that ye should earnestly contend for the faith which was once delivered to the saints. For there are certain men crept in unawares, who were before of old ordained to this condemnation; ungodly men, turning the grace of our God into lasciviousness, and denying the only Lord God, and our Lord Jesus Christ. I

THE CASE OF THE CENTURIES

will therefore put you in remembrance, though ye once knew this, how that the Lord, having saved the people out of the land of Egypt, afterward destroyed them that believed not. And the angels which kept not their first estate, but left their own habitation, he hath reserved in everlasting chains under darkness unto the judgement of the great day. Even as Sodom and Gomorrah, and the cities about them, in like manner, giving themselves over to fornication, and going after strange flesh, are set forth for an example, suffering the vengeance of eternal fire. Likewise these filthy dreamers defile the flesh, despise dominion, and speak evil of dignitaries. Yet Michael, when contending with the devil, he disputed about the body of Moses, durst not bring against him a railing accusation, but said, The Lord rebuke thee. But these speak evil of those things which they know not; but what they knew naturally as brute beasts, in those things they corrupt themselves. Woe unto them, for they have gone in the way of Cain, and ran greedily after the error of Balaam for reward,

WHAT IS A NIGGER

and perished in the gainsaying of Core."

Thus Jude, after stating various events, which occurred in the past, distinctly charges the people of Sodom and Gomorrah with giving themselves over to fornication, and going after strange flesh. And says that they are set for an example, suffering the vengenance of eternal fire. Continuing, Jude says: "These fifthy dreamers defile the flesh (this is precisely the offence with which God charged the antediluvians and the Canaanites), despise dominion (preferring social equality with the negro to that dominion which God designed them to have and commanded them to exercise), and speak evil of dignitaries."

In closing his charges against "these filthy dreamers, who defile the flesh by giving themselves over to fornication and going after strange flesh," Jude says: "Woe unto them! for they have gone in the way of Cain."

Thus the inspired apostle Jude, a New Testament writer, specifically charges that Cain was one of these filthy dreamers, who despise

THE CASE OF THE CENTURIES

dominion, defile the flesh, by giving themselves over to fornication, and going after strange flesh.

By comparing the sentence which God imposed upon Eve, and in which Adam was made a participant, with the sentence which he imposed upon Cain's paramour, and to which Cain was made a participant, we find that in each case the result to the parties interested was identical. The relation of husband and wife, which existed between Adam and Eve, was established in the days of their innocence, and was sanctioned by the law given man in the creation, "Be fruitful and multiply." But in their fallen state God saw fit, by special edict, to bind and comfine them in their sexual relations to each other, changing their former relations only so far as to place the offending woman in subjection to her husband, whom she had misled.

Lest we should be misunderstood upon this most important subject, we desire to state most emphatically that there is not a single passage of Scripture which warrants the slighest suspicion that either Adam or Eve ever descended

WHAT IS A NIGGER

to amalgamation. On the contrary, we are plainly taught that Cain led off in this wicked course. Hence, Jude describes it as "the way of Cain."

When Cain committed fornication with this female of strange flesh, he at once outraged the design of God in creating man and violated that Divine law given man in the Creation- "Have dominion • • • over every living thing that moveth upon the earth." "Dominion" means control, and control is the very opposite of social equality; and social equality, to a greater or less extent, is inseparable from sexual intercourse. And God in his wrath and disgust determined that he would visit upon Cain for his wanton, shameless, loathsome crime, the most degrading penalty. Thus, as in the case of Adam and Eve, God bound Cain and his paramour of strange flesh in the relation of husband and wife and confined them, in their sexual relations, to each other; and at the same time placed Cain's wife of strange flesh in subjection to him.

In the ordinary course of events, the first female born to the Adamic family, upon reaching

THE CASE OF THE CENTURIES

maturity, would have been given in marriage to Cain, the first born son. But Cain's shameless crime in cultivating sexual relations with a beast had rendered him unfit for the companionship of a pure woman. Besides, God's decree bound Cain in the relation of husband all his life long to this beast, and forever debarred him from holding sexual relations with women. Hence, the beautiful Adamic woman, who, in all her virgin loveliness, would have been the wife of Cain, would now become the wife of his brother, Abel. In his jealous rage upon realizing this, we might find an explanation of why "Cain rose up against Abel his brother and slew him."

The correctness of our interpretation of God's sentence upon Cain and his accomplice in sin-that it bound them together in the relation of husband and wife-is fully sustained by the scriptural record, which shows that subsequent to this event Cain is accredited with a wife, while prior to this event he is merely accredited with a paramour of strange flesh, with whom he committed fornication. The record is as follows:

WHAT IS A NIGGER

"And Cain went out from the presence of the Lord, and dwelt in the land of Nod, on the east of Eden. And Cain knew his wife, and she conceived and bare Enoch." (Gen. iv, 16-17.)

This scriptural record forms a part of a genealogical table, which shows the line of descent for five generations, and gives the name, occupation, etc., of the most prominent character in each generation of his descentants during that period of time.

We desire to call special attention to the fact that there is absolutely nothing in this record which indicates that Cain obtained his wife in the land of Nod. On the other hand, his previous history, as above shown, proves that she was formerly his paramour, and sustained that relation to him at the time when he and his brother Abel brought their offerings unto the Lord. And that, immediately after that event, God, by special decree, and as a punishment upon Cain for his criminal relations with her, bound them to each other in the relation of husband and wife. After their arrival in the land

THE CASE OF THE CENTURIES

of Nod, "Cain knew his wife," in the sense that she conceived and bare Enoch; just as, after their expulsion from the garden of Eden, "Adam knew Eve his wife," in the sense that she conceived and bare Cain. (See also Luke i, 36.) Cain and his wife disappear from the records, and all trace of them is lost after the birth of Enoch and the building of the city which Cain named after his son Enoch.

If, as many suppose, Cain had taken his sister to wife, sin would not have lain at his door as the result of his act. He would simply have obeyed the law given man in the creation: "Be fruitful and multiply." The only way the sons of Adam could have preserved and increased the pure Adamic flesh was by taking their sisters to wife. This course was evidently pursued by Seth and his younger brothers, and they were never censured for it. On the contrary, Seth, the third son of Adam, was very highly honored in that his taking his sister to wife placed his name in the line of descent from Adam to Jesus Christ. Hence, he stands in the genealogical tables of the Bible

WHAT IS A NIGGER

as one of the ancestors of the Messiah.

Thus, the testimony of the inspired writers, Moses, Jude and St. Paul, sweeps away the veil of mystery which for so many centuries, has enveloped the marital relations of Cain, and lays bare the most important and instructive events in his history, as follows:

1. That it was the sin which lay at Cain's door, which cost him the respect of God, and led to the rejection of his offering. The nature of his offering had no bearing on the result; any offering which he might have made would have shared the same fate. God had no respect for Cain as a man; hence, for his offering he had not respect.

2. That Cain had an associate in his crime.

3. That his associate in crime was a female.

4. That this female was not of the flesh of man; she was not a woman, but was a creature of strange flesh with which he was committing fornication. Just here, as in many other portions of the Bible, Paul's declaration that "There is one kind of flesh of men; another flesh of beast,

THE CASE OF THE CENTURIES

another of fishes, and another of birds," proves invaluable, in that it enables us to fathom many of the so-called mysteries of the Bible. When we turn it upon the statement of Jude that Cain was of those filthy dreamers who were guilty of giving themselves to fornication, and going after strange flesh, we can see at a glance that this creature with which Cain committed fornication was not of the flesh of man; that she was not a woman, but that she belonged to one of the three other kinds of flesh; and being a land animal, she necessarily belonged to the flesh of beasts. Hence, Cain's paramour was a beast.

5. That God in His wrath and digust at the depravity this displayed by Cain, in descending to sexual relations with a beast, bound Cain and his paramour of strange flesh in the relation of husband and wife, and confined their sexual relations to each other, thus forever debarring Cain from holding sexual relations with woman.

6. That Cain's wife of strange flesh conceived by him and bore him Enoch.

WHAT IS A NIGGER

7. That Cain's son Enoch, begotten of his wife of strange flesh, was indefinitely fertile; and that he had numerous descendants, children, grandchildren, great-grandchildren, etc.

8. That the descendants of Cain by his wife of strange flesh raised domestic animals, mined and worked metals and fashioned them into implements, and were skillful musicians, and for generations retained a knowledge of God and his dealings with Cain; and all circumstances indicate that they cultivated domestic plants, especially the food plants.

When called upon to identify this creature of strange flesh which bore Cain offspring as above described, science promptly invades the so-called human species, and points to the negro, the lowest of the so-called races of men, as the only creature among the lower kind of flesh with which man may associate himself carnally and produce offspring which will at once be indefinitely fertile and capable of being taught a knowledge of God and the arts of civilization.

Man's strong disposition to abandon

THE CASE OF THE CENTURIES

himself to this loathsome, destructive crime, as shown by his whole past history, is made even more conspicuous by the fact that Cain, the first child born to the Adamic creation, fell the victim of amalgamation.

The history of Cain and his descendants presents little to interest, and is practically of no value when viewed form the atheistic standpoint that man is a species divisible into races. But when viewed in the lights of revelation and the sciences, it is at once transformed into a subject of the most absorbing interest and importance. In the disasters which resulted to Cain from his association with his paramour of strange flesh, we find the most positive evidence of God's utter abhorrence of amalgamation; while in his formation and preservation of the genealogical table of Cain's descendants we find additional evidence of his unerring widsom, his infinite mercy, and of his wondrous love for man in thus making it a matter of scriptural record that there is a beast with which man may associate himself carnally and produce offspring, which will at

WHAT IS A NIGGER

once be indefinitely fertile and capable of acquiring a knowledge of God and of the arts of civilization.

Cain's wife being a negress, it follows that her offspring by Cain were mixed-bloods. This explains why Cain and his descendants were thrust out of the line of descent from Adam to the Saviour. Cain was the sole representative of the Adamic creation in his family. Hence, the only living soul, the last vestige of immortality in his family, disappeared when the spirit of Cain, whose crimes of murder and amalgamation made him a fugitive and a vagabond in time, took its flight from earth to receive the doom of the outcast in eternity.

The value of Paul's teaching that there are four different kinds of flesh is thus shown, in enabling us to see what Adam meant when he said: "Therefore shall a man leave his father and his mother and shall cleave unto his wife, and they shall be one flesh." In their ignorance of the true value of Paul's teaching, modern theologians have been led to believe that what Adam meant

THE CASE OF THE CENTURIES

was, that when a couple were joined in marriage, their respective individualities were merged to a certain extent and they became one in aspiration, interest, etc., or, as the Bible terms it, one flesh. But when viewed in the light of Paul's teaching as to flesh, and in the general teaching of the Bible that there is a beast with which man may associate himself carnally and produce offspring, we find that what Adam meant was, that the husband should not be of one "kind of flesh," and the wife of another "kind of flesh," they shall be one flesh; or, as Paul terms it, one "kind of flesh." And Cain and his wife were not of one flesh; they were of different kinds of flesh.

Further evidence that Cain's wife was not of the flesh of man-that she was not a woman-is found in the fact that Seth was the third child born to Adam, and took the place of Abel, whom Cain slew (Gen. iv, 25), and there were no daughters born to Adam until after the birth of Seth (Gen. iv, 4). Yet Cain had a wife before Seth was born. Thus, it is shown that Cain had a wife before there was a female child born to the

WHAT IS A NIGGER

Adamic family.

The degrading punishment which God visited upon Cain for his loathsome crime failed to deter other men from "going after strange flesh," as shown by the statement of Jude, as follows: "The angels which kept not their first estate, but left their own habitation * * * giving themselves over to fornication, and going after strange flesh * * * These filthy dreamers defile the flesh, despise dominion, and speak evil of dignitaries * * * Woe unto them, for they have gone in the way of Cain."

These "angels" were not celestial beings, but were creatures of flesh. They were the early descendants of Adam who went in the way of Cain. They "left their own habitation"-the Adamic flesh- "going after strange flesh;" that us, flesh that was of a different "kind of flesh" from their flesh. They "despised dominion," preferring social equality with the Negro to that "dominion" which God designed them to have, and commanded them to exercise. Such was the prevalence of amalgamation in the days of Enoch,

THE CASE OF THE CENTURIES

the seventh from Adam, that he warned the people that God would "execute judgement" upon them for their shameless violation of his law . (Jude.) Further evidence of the prevalence of this crime in antediluvian time is found in God's charge that "The sons of God saw the daughters of men that they were fair; and they took of them wives of all which they chose." (Gen. vi, 2.) The punishment-a universal deluge-which God visited upon the "sons of God" and "the daughters of men" and their progeny, proves that their relations were criminal. Hence, this text has been the subject of endless speculation. Men have even gone so far as to suppose that the "sons of God" were celestial beings-angels-who became enamored of the charms of the women of the earth- "the daughters of men"-and had intercourse with them, which resulted in producing offspring (see Lenormant's "Beginnings of History," chap. vii.). But, when we lay aside our atheism, and accept the teachings of scripture that man (the white) is a distinct creation, "in the image or God," and that the

WHAT IS A NIGGER

Negro is an ape, the mystery with which atheism has enveloped this text disappears, and, it becomes plain that "the sons of God" were the white males who traced their pedigree through a line of pure-blooded ancestors to Adam; and that "the daughters of men" were mixed-blood females who traced their pedigree to men, on the paternal side, and to negresses, on the maternal side. Their fathers were men, but their mothers were negresses-apes-beasts. Hence, the unions between the male descendants of Adam and these mixed-blooded females resulted in further corrupting the flesh of the earth, and finally led God in His wrath and disgust to destory them with the deluge as shown by the following:

"And God saw that the wickedness of man was great in the earth, and every imagination of the thoughts of his heart was only evil continually. And it repented the Lord that he had made man on the earth, and it grieved him at his heart. And the Lord said, I will destroy man whom I have created from the face of the earth; both man and beast, and the creeping things, and the fowls of

THE CASE OF THE CENTURIES

the air; for it repenteth me that I have made them." (Gen. vi, 5-6-7.)

But just at this critical juncture, the most critical that man has ever known, when the hand of the Almighty God was raised in his just wrath to destroy from the earth which their shameless crime had corrupted the last vestige of the seed of man, "Noah found grace in the eyes of the Lord." (Gen. vi, 8.) Why? "Noah was a just man and perfect in his generations, and Noah walked with God." (Gen. vi, 9.)

It will be observed that there are three characteristics here recorded of Noah, which are assigned as so many reasons why "Noah found grace in the eyes of the Lord:" (1) "Noah was a just man;" (2) he was "perfect in his generations;" (3) "Noah walked with God." The first and third characteristics are happily not uncommon, for in sacred history various individuals are accredited with similar characteristics. The second characteristic is common to every pure-blooded descendant of Adam. But the record of it, unlike the choracitic itself, is peculiar to Noah. It is not

WHAT IS A NIGGER

significant that in all sacred history there is just this one individual of whom it is recorded in just so many words that he was "perfect in his generations?" No such record is found of Abraham, the father of all Isarel; nor of Moses, the great law-giver of Isarel; nor of David, the sweet singer of Isarel; nor even of the Messiah. This characteristic in Noah, that he was "perfect in his generations," was not the result of any act upon his part; and all credit for his possession of it is due solely to his ancestors, who transmitted to him from Adam in uncorrupted line of descent the pure Adamic stock. This characteristic assigned as one of the reasons why "Noah found grace in the eyes of the Lord," with its attendant circumstances, necessarily carries with it the implication that there were others in Noah's day who were not perfect in their generations. Now, if Noah was "perfect in his generations" because his ancestors transmitted to him from Adam in uncorrupted line of descent the pure Adamic stock, and there were others in Noah's day who were not perfect in their generations, by

THE CASE OF THE CENTURIES

association with whom did their ancestors transmit to them a corrupted line of descent from Adam? The morals of man may be corrupted by illicit intercourse between the sexes, but the offspring will be of pure Adamic stock, whether the relations of its parents are legitimate or otherwise. Hence, as long as man's sexual relations are confined to the Adamic family-to the "flesh of men"-their genealogy will be "perfect," and the line of descent uncorrupted. This being true, it follows that the genealogy or the antediluvians-their line of descent from Adam-could only have been corrupted by their sexual relations with some other "kind of flesh." which resulted in the production of offspring that was indefinitely fertile.

While the most depraved conditions of their morals is implied in his arraignment of them, the sole charge of the Almighty against the descendants of Adam in Noah's day, is, that under their administration the flesh of the earth was corrupted." "The earth also was corrupt before God, and the earth was filled with violence,

WHAT IS A NIGGER

And God looked upon the earth, and behold it was corrupt; for all flesh had corrupted his way on the earth." (Gen. vi, 11-12.)

This term "all flesh" suggests to our mind the inquiry as to how many kinds of flesh there are on the earth, and what in God's eye would constitute the difference between them. An intelligent reply demands that we turn upon this record the inspired light of Paul's declaration that "there is one kind of flesh of men, another flesh of beasts, another of fishes, and another of birds," making in all four distinct kinds of flesh; and then turn upon it the inspired light of the Mosaic Record, which teaches that the fish were made to inhabit the waters; that the fowl were made to fly above the earth in the open expanse of heaven, and that man and the beasts were made to inhabit the dry land. We are thus taught that there are just two kinds of flesh on the earth, which belong strictly to the earth-the flesh of man and the flesh of beasts. As has been shown, no form of lust which man can indulge within the pale of the Adamic family can corrupt the flesh

THE CASE OF THE CENTURIES

of man. However illicit the unions, the offspring is of pure Adamic flesh, unadulterated by any foreign element. The same rule holds good with the beasts. No hybridization which may occur between the different species or races of beasts can corrupt the flesh of beasts. The offspring resulting from these unions is the pure flesh of beasts, unadulterated by any foreign element. To corrupt the flesh there must be sexual contact between two different kinds of flesh; and the "corrupted" flesh must express itself in the offspring. Hence, in discussing this question we should bear in mind that however loathsome the lust, no corruption of the flesh can result to the participants in it. To illustrate: The flesh of man is a kind of flesh distinct from that of beasts, while the Negro, being merely a race of the ape species, belongs to the flesh of beasts. Now, let a man associate himself carnally with a negress; the flesh of that man is not corrupted by his contact with that beast, neither is the flesh of the beast corrupted by her contact with the man; the flesh of each is as pure after the contact as it was

WHAT IS A NIGGER

before. But when the contact results in conception and birth, the corrupted flesh which is the sole charge of the Almighty against the antediluvians, expresses itself in the offspring-in the mulatto-which is not born the pure flesh of man, as was its Adamic parent, neither is it the pure flesh of beast, as was its parent the negress; it is what God so fitly describes it as being corrupted flesh, resulting from amalgamation between the flesh of man and the flesh of beast. Further evidence that there is a beast with which man may associate himself carnally, and produce offspring, is found in God's law to Isreal, in which is assigned his reasons for the destruction of the Canaanites. After enumerating and forbidding every form of illicit sexual intercourse which it is possible for man to indulge within the pale of the Adamic family, God closes his law on the subject as follows: "Neither shalt thou lie with any beast to defile thyself therewith; neither shall any woman stand before a beast to lie down thereto; it is confusion. (Lev. xviii.:23.) Confusion, mixing, mingling, are synonymous

THE CASE OF THE CENTURIES

terms. Hence, there should be no mixing, no mingling, no confusion of man's blood with that of a beast.

Continuing, God said: "Defile not ye yourselves in any of these things; for in all these the nations are defiled which I cast out before you; and the land is defiled; therefore I do visit the iniquity thereof upon it; and the land itself vomiteth out its inhabitants. Ye shall therefore keep my statutes and my judgements, and not commit any of these abomination. * * * That the land spue not you out also when ye defile it, as it spued out the nations that were before you." (Lev. xviii, 24, 25, 26, 28.)

A careful investigation of the laws of God will demonstrate that the violation of this statute forbidding man to lie with a beast is the only crime that man can commit that will have the three results described in the narrative of the deluge and that of the Canaanites: (1) The corruption of flesh; (2) the corruption of the earth itself in the eyes of God; (3) the penalty of death under the law of God. Prior to the deluge,

WHAT IS A NIGGER

God looked upon the earth and said it was corrupt; for all flesh had corrupted his way upon the earth. God thus describes a condition of the flesh of the earth, which could only have resulted from amalgamation. Prior to the arrival of the Israelites in Canaan, God said of the land of Canaan, "The land is defiled." Defile and corrupt are synonymous terms. He specifically charges the Canaanites with lying with beasts, which, as shown in the case of the antediluvians, would result in corrupting the flesh of Canaan. In each case the penalty of death was visited upon this corrupted flesh and those who were instrumental in corrupting it. In the case of the antediluvians by a universal deluge; in that of the Canaanites by a war of extermination.

Thus, to accept the teachings of the Bible, we must admit that there is a beast with which man may associate himself carnally and produce a fertile offspring. As we have shown, the teachings of science prove the Negro an ape; and all history and all scientific research and all observation combine to teach us that the Negro

THE CASE OF THE CENTURIES

is the only one of the lower animals with which man may associate himself carnally and produce a fertile offspring. Hence, we have no alternative than to decide that it was their criminal relations with the negro which brought the curses of God upon the antediluvians and the Canaanites and led to their destruction by Divine edict.

Nothing could place God in a more ridiculous light than to suppose that He enacted a statute forbidding man to commit, and then, as if to emphasize the absurdity, to affix the death penalty to the violation of the law. Hence, if we accept the Bible as the expression of God's will to man, we have no alternative than to decide that the very presence of this Divine law forbidding man to "lie with a beast," or a woman "to lie down thereto," proves the existence of a beast which a man may lie with just as he would with a woman; or to which a woman, if she desired carnal association with, might lie down to just as she would to a man. Had this great law of God's been obeyed, no mulatto would ever have "defiled" this beautiful earth with his

WHAT IS A NIGGER

presence; a presence at once degrading to man and loathsome to God; or had the just penalty which God attached to the violation of his law been enforced, no mulatto would have lived to see the light of day: "And if a man lie with a beast, he shall surely be put to death, and ye shall slay the beast. And if a woman approach unto any beast and lie down thereto, thou shalt kill the woman and the beast; they shall surely be put to death; their blood shall be upon them." (Lev. xx, 15-16.) Which is equivalent to God's saying to man, "Have no superstitious fears that their blood will be upon your hands, no conscientious scruples that their blood will be upon your head; kill them for their shameless violation of Divine law; slay them in obedience to Divine command-their blood shall be upon them."

Thus, the immediate offspring of man and the Negro-the mulatto-was doomed by Divine edict to instant death in the very moment of conception. Hence, neither the mulatto nor his ultimate offspring can acquire the right to live. This being true, it follows that these monstrosities

THE CASE OF THE CENTURIES

have no rights social, financial, political or religious that man need respect; they have no rights that man dare respect-not even the right to live. We find an illustration of this in God's command to Israel to "utterly destroy" the Canaanites of all ages and sexes, and "leave nothing alive that breatheth," and take their country with its accumulated wealth of ages. The offspring of Man and the Negro is not upon the earth in deference to Divine will, but in violation of Divine law. Hence, it is not a part of God's creation. And there can never be any peace between God and man so long as this corrupted flesh is permitted to "defile" the earth with its presence. Inasmuch as the immediate offspring of Man and the Negro is corrupted flesh, it follows that its ultimate offspring could never become pure. If mated continuously with pure whites for millions of generations, you could never breed the ape out, nor breed the spiritual creation in, the offspring of man and the Negro. It was not a part of God's creation to begin with, and could never become so. Surely

WHAT IS A NIGGER

the great Architect of the universe has not become so imbecile, His creative power so far waned, that he must needs accept and appropriate to himself this loathsome product of His creatures' crime.

THE CASE OF THE CENTURIES

Chapter VI.
Red, Yellow and Brown Skin Denoted Amalgamation of the Human Family with the Beast, the Negro.

The mere fact that, under the influence of the law of heredity, the ultimate offspring of whites and negroes, when mated continuously with whites, present to a greater or less extent the elevated physical and mental characters of the white, does not make them men and women. They lack the spiritual creation, which forms the link of kinship between God and man, and is only transmitable to his offspring through pure Adamic channels. Nothing could be more absurd, nothing more blasphemous, than to suppose that God, who declined to establish any kinship between himself and the animals, would make it possible for man to do so, by an act, which of itself, is a violation of that devine law, "Thou shalt not lie with any beast." Hence, the mixed-

WHAT IS A NIGGER

bloods, the corrupted flesh, inherit none of the immortality of their Adamic parent-they have no soul. But, like the negro, and the rest of the animals, they are merely combinations of matter and mind. They were not in existence at the time of Adam's transgression; and are not included in the Plan of Salvation. Man alone fell, and he alone is the subject of redemption. Hence, "Go ye into all the world, and preach the gospel to every creature." (Mark xvi.:15.) Remembering that God "hath made of one blood all nations of men." (Acts xvii.:26.) But, "Give not that which is holy unto the dogs, neither cast ye your pearls before swine, lest they trample them under their feet, and turn again and rend you." (Matt. vii.:6)

The existence of this prohibitory statute demonstrates the existence of an animal which man, in his criminal ignorance of God's plan of creation, might mistake for a man, and thus be misled into giving him the Bible with the view of conferring upon him the blessings of Christianity, which were intended alone for man. When we view this statute in the light of the sciences, and

THE CASE OF THE CENTURIES

in that of Paul's declaration that "there is one kind of flesh of men, another flesh of beasts," etc., it becomes plain that the dog, the swine and the negro all belong to one kind of flesh-the flesh of beasts. The scriptures are described "holy" (Rom. i, 2, etc.) The kingdom of heaven compared to "goodly pearls" (Matt. xiii, 45-46). Hence,, we are led to decide that "that which is holy," and which man is forbidden to "give unto dogs," is the Bible. And that the pearls which man is forbidden to cast before swine is the kingdom of heaven. This statue was evidently designed to confine the use of the Bible and religious worship to man, and exclude the lower kinds of flesh, which embrace the negro. Hence, if it is criminal to give the Bible to dogs, it is criminal to give it to the negro; if it is criminal to undertake to Christianize swine, it is criminal to undertake to christianize the negro. In these respects man can make no distinction between one animal and another. This prohibitory law applies with equal force to the mixed-bloods; they possess none of the spiritual creation, but

WHAT IS A NIGGER

are wholly animal. The "heathen" to whom the Saviour commanded that the gospel should be preached were the pure-blooded decendants of Adam, who had lost their knowledge of the true God, and of all religious worship, or had descended to idolatry.

The Saviour's decree, "Go ye into the world, and preach the gospel to every creature,: that is, to every creature for whom it was designed, was fully executed. Paul says that in his day the gospel "was preached to every creature which is under heaven." (Col. i, 23). This sweeping statement of the learned apostle was either true or false. We accept it as unquestionably true. The gospel reached all for whom it was intended. Yet it was not preached to the wild tribes of negroes and mixed-bloods of Africa; nor to the Laplanders, Finns, and Basques of Europe; nor to the Hindoos, Coreans, Chinese, Japanese, etc., of Asia; nor to the Australians, Malays, etc., of Oceanica; nor to the wild, hunting tribes of North and South America; nor to the Mexicans, Peruvians, etc. And no well-informed

THE CASE OF THE CENTURIES

man or woman will assert that it was. This being true, it follows that Paul either misrepresented the facts when he said that in his day the gospel "was preached to every creature which is under heaven," or the Negroes, Hindoos, Chinese, Malays, Indians, Basques, etc., are not included in the Plan of Salvation.

If the gospel, as "published" by the primitive church, was confined to the pure white, and was not preached to the negro and the so-called "brown, red an yellow races" of the earth, where does the modern church obtain its authority to extend it to them? The explanation is simple. The primitive church which our Saviour established found its ultimate basis on the scriptural narrative of Divine creation, which teaches that man [the white] is a distinct creation "in the image of God." The modern church finds its ultimate basis on the atheistic theory of Natural Development, which teaches that man is a highly developed species of ape-the human species-of which the white is the highest, and the Negro, Malay, Indian and Monogolian are lower races

WHAT IS A NIGGER

of men. Thus, it is clear that the modern Christian church derives its authority for recognizing the negro, the Indian, Malay, Chinese, etc., as lower races of men and for extending the gospel to them, not from scripture, but from atheism. The idea that the church can "present" these base-born mixed-bloods, "perfect in Christ Jesus," when their very existence is alone traceable to the most shameless violation of Divine law! This modern church theory that the negro and the mixed-bloods are included in the Plan of Salvation is another result of putting man and the ape in the same family.

When, in antediluvian times, amalgamation had corrupted the flesh of earth, God decided to destory "all flesh," save Noah, "and they that were with him in the ark." Thus, the flesh of the earth was restored to its original purity. This illustrious family brought with them from their antediluvtan home, and transmitted to their descendants a knowledge of the arts and sciences which had been accumulating in the Adamic family for ages. This explains why the

THE CASE OF THE CENTURIES

most ancient artisans were the most skillful and accomplished, as shown by the fact that their architectural remains are invariably the most superb. Mr. Taylor says: "Among the ancient cultured nations of Egypt and Assyria, handicrafts had already come to a stage which could only have been reached by thousands of years of progress. In museums still may be examined the work of their joiners, stonecutters, goldsmiths, wonderful in skill and finish, and often putting to shame the modern artificer. * * * To see gold jewelry of the highest order, the student should examine that of the ancients, such as the Egyptian, Greek and Etruscan." (Anthropology.)

At the close of the deluge, Noah and his family settled upon one of the continents, and, with their negroes, proceeded to build for themselves homes, and in the course of time developed a great civilization. Having grown rich and populous, their descendants threw off colonies onto other continents. These colonists carried with them their negroes and other

WHAT IS A NIGGER

domestic animals, domestic plants, metallic implements, and all the appliances of civilized life, and in the course of time developed the splendid civilizations, the remains of which are found upon every continent of the earth, and which even in their ruins command the admiration of the modern world. When we turn upon these ancient civilizations the light of modern science, we find that they were the work of the white-that "no negro civilization has ever appeared; no Monogolian one has been highly developed." The white "is pre-eminently the man of civilization." The extent and splendor of their architectural remains indicate that those ancient whites who, with their negroes, developed those great civilizations, must have numbered their populations by the hundreds of millions. What became of them? What became of all those hundred of millions of white-skinned, silken-haired whites? They have long since disappeared from three of the five continents, leaving no progeny of white-skinned, silken-haired whites. The remnant of their white descendants are

THE CASE OF THE CENTURIES

practically confined to portions of Europe and America. What became of all those hundreds of millions of black-skinned, wooly-haired negroes? They have long since disappeared from four of the five continents, leaving no progeny of black-skinned, wooly-haired negroes. The remnant of their pure-blooded descendants have dwindled down to a few tribes in Africa. And where did all those so-called "brown, red and yellow races of men" come from, which we find in possession of these ancient civilizations, and which, in the sum of their physical and mental characters, are identical with the known offspring of whites and negroes in our midst? These degraded, worthless creatures never developed the civilizations which they possess, and as a rule they have no knowledge of who their builders were. Many of the ruins of the most magnificent civilizations are found in districts which are now occupied by wild, hunting tribes of savages.

The so-called "brown, red and yellow races" have no characters peculiar to them. No anthropologist will assert that the classification

WHAT IS A NIGGER

of the so-called "human species" into "five races of men" was based upon what the atheist would term "racial purity," but that it was based solely on geographical divisions. In Europe, the complexions range from pure white to brown; in Africa, we find the complexions to be nearly white, brown, red, yellow and pure black; in Asia, they range from light yellow to black; the same is true of Oceanica, the home of the so-called "Malay race;" in America, previous to its discovery by Columbus, the complexions were nearly pure white, brown, red, yellow and black. Fontaine says: "If a congregation of twelve representatives from Malacca, China, Japan. Mongolia, Sandwich Islands, Chili, Peru, Brazil, Chickasaws, Comanches, etc., were dressed alike, or undressed and unshaven, the most skillful anatomist could not, from their appearance, separate them." [How the World Was Peopled.]

Prof. Winchell says: "The ancient Indians of California, in the latitude of 42 degrees, were as black as the negroes of Guines, while in Mexico were tribes of an olive or reddish

THE CASE OF THE CENTURIES

complexion, relatively light. Among the black races of tropical regions we find, generally, some light-colored tribes interspersed. These sometimes have light hair and blue eyes. This is the case with the Tuareg of the Sahara, the Afghans of India, and the aborigines of the banks of the Orinoco and the Amazon." [*Preademites.*] It will be observed that these characters are identical with those presented by the offspring resulting from amalgamation between whites and blacks in our midst. We have demonstrated here in the United States that the way to produce these so-called "brown, red or yellow races" is to mingle the blood of the white with that of the negro.

Let us take a hasty glance at the conditions presented by the continent of America upon its discovery by Columbus! There existed here the remains of an ancient civilization which extended from New York to Chili and from ocean to ocean. While some of its cities and villages were preserved and occupied, its greatest and most ancient cities were abandoned and in ruins.

WHAT IS A NIGGER

Mr. Donnelly says of Gran-Chimu: "Its remains exist today, the wonder of the southern continent, covering not less than twenty square miles, Tombs, temples and palaces arise on every hand, ruined but still traceable. Immense pyramidal structures, some of them half a mile in circuit; vast areas shut in by massive walls, each containing its water-tank, its shops, municipal edifices, and the dwellings of its inhabitants, and each a branch of a larger organization; prisons, furnaces for smelting metals, and almost every concomitant of civilization existed in the ancient Chimu capital. One of the pyramids, called the "Temple of the Sun," is 812 feet long by 470 wide and 150 high. These vast structures have been in ruins for centuries." [*Atlantis.*]

Such competent judges as Stevens, Dupaix, and Charnay pronounce the architectural remains of Central America to be equal, in point of solidity, beauty and finish, to those of Egypt, Rome or Greece in their best days. "The Peruvians made large use of aqueducts, which they built with notable skill, using hewn stone

THE CASE OF THE CENTURIES

and cement, and making them very substantial. One extended four hundred and fifty miles across sierras and over rivers. * * * The public roads of the Peruvians were most remarkable; they were built of masonry. One of these roads ran along the mountains through the whole length of the empire, from Quito to Chili; another, starting from this at Cuzco, went down to the coast, and extended northward to the equator. These roads were from twenty to twenty-five feet wide, were macadamized with pulverized stone mixed with lime and bituminous cement, and were walled in by strong walls more than a fathom in thickness. In many places these roads were cut for leagues through the rock; great ravines were filled up with solid masonry; rivers were crossed by suspension bridges, used here ages before their introduction in Europe." [*Ibid.*]

The ancient Americans, like their brethren of other continents, built great mounds and truncated pyramids of earth, upon which to erect their magnificent palaces and temples; these were frequently from 50 to 100 feet high, and

WHAT IS A NIGGER

sometimes covered several acres. "The pyramid of Cholula is one of the greatest constructions ever erected by human hands. It is, even now, in its ruined condition, 160 feet high, 1,400 feet square at the base, and covers forty-five acres; we have only to remember that the greatest pyramid of Egypt-Cheops-covers but twelve or thirteen acres, to form some conception of the magnitude of this American structure." (*Ibid.*)

Our limited space forbids the mention of many other evidence of the enlightenment of the ancient Americans. But we have the most postitive evidence that it was the work of whites, who, with their negroes, occupied this continent in the remote past.

(1) "Of the predecessors of the Toltecs in Mexico, the Olmecs and Xicalancans were the most important. They were the forerunners of the great races that followed. According to Ixtilxochitl, 'they came from the east in ships and barks.'" (*Ibid.*)

(2) "On the monuments of Central America there are representations of bearded

THE CASE OF THE CENTURIES

men. How could the beardless American Indians have imagined a bearded race?" (*Ibid.*)

(3) Quelyatcoatl, the leader of the Nahuas, and who was deified, is described as having been a white man, with strong formation of body, broad forehead, large eyes and flowing beard. (*Ibid.*)

(4) "Very ancient ruins, showing remains of large and remarkable edifices, were found near Huamanga, and described by Ciera de Leon. The native traditions said this city was built by bearded white men, who came there long before the time of the Incas and established a settlement." [*Ibid.*]

"Prof. Wilson describes the hair of the ancient Peruvians, as found upon their mummies, as 'a lightish brown and of a fineness of texture which equals that of the Anglo-Saxon race.'" [*Ibid.*]

Short says: "The ancient Peruvians appear, from numerous examples of hair found in their tombs, to have been an auburn-haired race." [*North Americans of Antiquity.*]

WHAT IS A NIGGER

Haywood says that in the early part of the century three mummies were found in a cave on the south side of the Cumberland river (Tennessee) who were buried in baskets as the Peruvians generally buried; their skin was white and their hair auburn and of a fine texture. (*Natural and Aboriginal History of Tennessee.*)

[5] Desare Charnay has published in the North American Review for December, 1880, photographs of a number of idols exhumed at San Juan de Trotihaucan, "which show striking negroid faces." [*Atlantis.*]

The Popol Vuh, the ancient book of the Quiches, refers to a period of great peace in the remote past, when the whites and blacks "lived together" and "all seem to have spoken one language." [*Bancroft's Native Races.*]

This harmonizes with the teaching of Scripture that there was a period in the remote past when "the whole earth was of one language and one speech." During this period the black servant spoke the language of his white master. This statement of ther Popol Vuh indicates that

THE CASE OF THE CENTURIES

during this period of great peace, the whites and the blacks were the only inhabitants of the earth; no browns, reds or yellows are mentioned, which they certainly would have been had they then existed. It also indicates that the Popol Vuh was written by some ancient white. How could the so-called "red men" know anything of whites and blacks? The history of every nationality of ancient time, sustained by our experience with the Negro in the United States, demonstrates that the White must be the master of the Negro, else they can never live together in peace. This is the law of God. And it has cost every nationality of ancient times its existence to violate it. That, during this period of "great peace," the ancient whites, who, with their negroes, developed the splendid civilization of America, respected the law of God and maintained the relation of master and servant which God established between Man and the Negro in the Creation, is shown by the following:

Dr. Le Plongeon says: "Besides the sculptures of long-bearded men seen by the

WHAT IS NIGGER

explorer at Chichen Itza, there were tall figures of people with small heads, thick lips and curly, short hair or wool, regarded as negroes. * * * We always see them as standard or parasol bearers, but never engaged in actual warfare." [*Maya Archaeology.*]

Thus, it is shown that, in that remote sage, the Negro was simply a menial. When America was discovered by Europeans in modern times, these ancient whites and their negroes had disappeared from the earth; their civilization was in ruins; their once fertile fields were transformed into a wilderness-a "desolalation"- the abode of colored barbarians and savages. Upon the discovery of these creatures, the atheist pronouned them a new and "lower race of men," which had descended from the ape, and attributed their degraded condition to arrested development. The Christians of the world promptly proceeded to hasten the development of this new-found "race of men" by civilizing, educating and Christianing them, In this violation of Divine law they lost many a scalp, but never saved a

THE CASE OF THE CENTURIES

soul.

Dr. Morton, an early writer upon the subject, misled the world into believing that the so-called "Indian race" possessed certain peculiar characteristics; that they were red or copper-colored men, with high cheek-bones, prominent noses, small black eyes, thin lips, with hair straight, coarse and black. The "Mortonian Theory" has long since been exploded, yet it is persistently taught to the youth of the country. The Indian has no character peculiar to him; even the red or copper color is found in Africa. [Anthropology.] And it is significant that it is occasionally found among our mulattoes.

Catlin says: "A stranger in the Mandan village is first struck with the different shades of complexion and various colors of hair which he sees in a crowd about him, and is at once disposed to exclaim, 'These are not Indians.' There are a great many of these people whose complexions appear as light as half-breeds; and among the women particularly there are many whose skins are almost white, with the most pleasing

WHAT IS A NIGGER

symmetry and proportion of feature; with hazel, with gray, and with blue eyes. * * * Among the females may be seen every shade and color of hair that can be seen in our country, except red or auburn. * * * There are very many of both sexes, and of every age, from infancy to manhood and old age, with hair of a bright, silvery gray, and in some instances perfectly white. * * * And by passing this hair through my hands I have found it uniformly to be as coarse and harsh as a horse's mane, differing materially from the hair of other colors, which, among the Mendans, is generally as fine and soft as silk." [Indians of North America.]

Prichard says: "It will be easy to show that the American races show nearly as great a variety in this respect as the nations of the old continent; there are among them white races with florid complexions, and tribes and countenance are almost equally diversified." [Researches into the Physical History of Mankind.]

Short says: "The Menominees, sometimes

THE CASE OF THE CENTURIES

called the 'White Indians,' formerly occupied the region bordering on Lake Michigan, Green Bay. The whiteness of these Indians, which is compared to that of white mulattoes, early attracted the attention of the Jesuit missionaries, and has often been commented on by travelers. Almost every shade, from the ash-color of the Menominees, through the cinnamon red, copper, and bronze tints, may be found among the tribes formerly occupying the territory east of the Mississippi, until we reach the dark-skinned Kaws of Kansas, who are nearly as black as the negro. The variety of complexion is as great in South America as among the tribes of the northern part of the continent." [*North Americans of Antiquity.*]

Thus, we find that in the remote past, this continent was settled by whites, who, with their negroes, developed a great civilization; then both whites and negroes disappeared; their civilization crumbled into ruins, and their country became a wilderness-the abode of barbarians and savages, which, in their physical and mental characters,

WHAT IS A NIGGER

are identical with the offspring of whites and negroes in our midst.

Let us bear in mind that there are just two schools of learning which propose to explain the phenomena of the universe, of which these so-called "Malay, Indian, and Mongolian races," are a part; and that these are the schools of Divine Creation, and Natural Development, respectively. Hence, we have no alternative than to decide that these so-called "Brown, Red, and Yellow races," have developed from the ape, and present so many cases of "arrested development;" or we must decide that, they are the result of amalgamation between the whites and the negroess of ancient time, just as the browns, reds, and yellows in our midst, are the result of amalgamation between the whites and negroes of modern times. How many ways are there of producing these creatures? Are we to understand that, in the remote past, the same class of creatures were produced by development from the ape, that we now produce by amalgamation between whites and negroes?

THE CASE OF THE CENTURIES

Many of these mixed-blooded nations, such as these Chinese, Hindoos, Egyptians, etc., have preserved more or less of the literature of their white ancestors. A careful investigation of their literature reveals the fact that their remote ancestors were monotheists (see the works of Renouf, Wilkerson, Rawlinson, Legge, Clark, Max Muler.) This should occasion us no surprise. Monotheism was the religion of Noah; and was handed down to his descendants. Yet, in every instance, their mixed-blooded descendants, when found far removed from the influenee of the whites, have either lost all knowledge of a God, and of religious worship, or they have descended to idolatry.

Previous to the creation of man, the negro had no more idea of a God, or of religious worship, than any other animal. But God established between himself and man, the tie of kinship, which forms a bond of love and sympathy between them, and enables man to respect, confide in, and worship an all-wise, all-powerful, but invisible God. But no kinship exists between

WHAT IS A NIGGER

God and the mixed-bloods. Hence, though these creatures may inherit from their Adamic ancestors a knowledge of God, when relieved of the influence of the white, they soon lose all confidence in, and all respect for, an invisible God. They must have a god which they can see; and in the absence of such an one, they fashion for themselves gods of wood, stone, or metal; or deify some animate, or inanimate object, as their whim suggests. Thus, amalgamation becomes the parent of idolatry. Hayti furnishes an illustration of this. In 1793, the negroes were emancipated. In 1825, England formally acknowledged the republic of Hayti. Thus, this fine country was turned over to the negroes and mixed bloods. They were given an organized system of political gevernment, and an organized system of religion; with churches, schools, and all the appliances of civilization; yet despite the most persistent efforts of Catholics and Protestants, to hold them up to a civilized life, they have descended to fetish worship and cannibalism, in the shadow of scores of churches.

THE CASE OF THE CENTURIES

They sacrifice their own offspring to snakes, and then eat the sacrifice; the ceremonies ending in a drunken debauch, which is characterized by the most indiscriminate intercourse between the sexes. (Sir Spencer St. John, *Hayti; or the Black Republic.*)

This reveals the startling truth that, underlying all of God's arraignments, and punishments of Isreal, and her surrounding nations, for their idolatry, was this loathsome crime, amalgamation. It is not the idol, nor his confidence in it, but the obscene rites, and the indiscriminate intercourse between the sexes, which usually characterizes the worship of idols that induces man to renounce God, abandon his worship, and embrace idolatry. Their children are reared in a cess-pool of amalgamation, and trained to worship idols. Hence, in the course of time, they lose all knowledge of the true God, and of his worship, and become "heathen."

Man's social, political, and religious equality with the negro, inevitably leads to amalgamation; and this, in its turn, gives birth to

WHAT IS A NIGGER

idolatry; then, in order to get the negro and his amalgamated progeny into the family of man, the truth of Divine Creation is repudiated; and the Theory of Evolution is substituted in its stead. It was his desire to counteract the results of these destructive crimes, which led God to "raise up" for himself "a chosen people," in the Israelites, who would be "peculiar," in that they they would not descend to amalgamation and idolatry; and in order to disabuse their minds of, and counteract the degrading influences of the Theory of Evolution, which was universally taught in that day, God gave to Isreal the Narrative of Creation, together with a history of the events which led up to the Isrealitish occupancy of Canaan. It was God's desire that Isreal would lead all men to renounce atheism, and abandon amalgamation and idolatry. But instead of respecting and executing the will of God, the Israelites abandoned themselves to the crimes they were designed to eradicate. Then God sent prophets to warn them of the results of their wicked course, and visited upon them war,

THE CASE OF THE CENTURIES

pestilence, famine, etc., to induce them to return to their allegiance to him. Then, as a last resort, he sent the Savior, who established the Christian church on the Narrative of Creation. But evidently the primitive Christian church, which eliminated the negro and the mixed-bloods, did not long survive the Savior. For many centuries the modern church has found its ultimate basis on the Theory of Development; the negro and the mixed-bloods are recognized as "lower races of men," and the gospel extended to them; and both the clergy and laity of to-day, are doing all in their power, socially, politcally, and religiously, to perpetuate on this earth a condition of affairs, which our Savior died to put an end to.

All the facts indicate that, for a long period, the descentdants of Noah respected the design of God, in creating man; lived in obedience to his laws, and maintained the relation of master and servant, which God established between man and the negro, in the Creation. During this period, described in the "Popol Vuh" as one of "great peace," they prospered and were happy in

WHAT IS A NIGGER

the approving smile of heaven; and developed upon the various continents, the most superb civilizations. But, in an evil hour, they violated the law God, by descending to amalgamation with their negroes; and the smiles of heaven were exchanged for its frowns; the blessings of God were withdrawn, and his curses were showered upon them in the forms of war, famine, pestilence, etc., to induce them to abandon their wicked course, and return to their duties. But, like the antediluvians, they persisted in their evil way; nation after nation was destroyed from the face of the earth, their civilizations laid in ruins, and their country turned over to the barbarians and savages their crime had produced.

These ancient people left in their great cities, sumptuous palaces, magnificent temples, gigantic pyramids, etc., the most enduring evidences of their enlightenment. But, when amalgamation has absorbed, and destroyed us, as it absorbed and destroyed them, what evidence will we leave to the explorers of thirty or forty centuries hence, that we were a great agricultural,

THE CASE OF THE CENTURIES

commercial, and maritime people; that in eager quest of other avenues of trade, our ships had rode the billows of every ocean, and touched the shores of every continent of the earth? Absolutely none. Our frail civilization, of which we so highly boast, will disappear under the destructive influences of a few centuries, aided by the vandal hand of the savages we are producing, like mist before the morning sun; scarcely a vestige will remain. Hence, when we make monotheism, a knowledge of the arts and sciences, the number and magnitude of mechanical structures, the skill displayed in their construction, and their durability, the test of enlightened civilizations, we must admit that the great architects of these ancient civilizations were at least out peers.

In discussing the subject, we should carefully consider the stealthfulness with which amalgamation accomplishes its destructive results. This crime always begins between the white males and the black females. Quatrefages says: "In the crossings between unequal human races, the father almost always belongs to the

WHAT IS A NIGGER

superior race. In every case, and especially in transient amours, woman refuses to lower herself; man is less delicate." (The Human Species.) Thus, it is evident that the mixed-bloods must rapidly increase at the expense of both the pure whites, and the pure negroes. Upon reaching maturity, a very considerable percentage of the mixed-bloods, males and females, will take mates from among the negroes; again, many Adamic males will take concubines from among both negroes and mixed-bloods. Thus, the negro becomes the prey, not only of the white males, but also of the mix-bloods of both males and female. Hence, it is easy to see that it is simply a question of time, when the negro will be absorded and destroyed, and their descendants will all be mixed-bloods. This has been demonstrated in the United States. The first negroes from Africa, were imported here in A. D., 1619. Amalgamation at once began, to-day there is not a pure-blooded negro on this continent. Not one. Now it only remains for the mixed-bloods to complete the absorption and

THE CASE OF THE CENTURIES

destruction of the pure whites, and we will leave this continent as we found it, populated with mixed-bloods. Hence, when we disabuse our minds of the atheism, which teaches that the white and the negro are but different races of the same species of animal, and accept the scriptural teaching, that they are different kinds of flesh, the progeny resulting from their unions appears in a very different light.

Woman, the female side, or part of man, is the great stronghold, the vital point, of the Adamic Creation. Hence, as long as the marriage relations of the pure Adamic females of a nation, or continent, is confined to pure Adamic males, the pure Adamic stock of that nation, or continent, cannot be absorbed and destroyed by amalgamation. In addition to their Adamic wives, the Adamic males will, here and there, have negro concubines. From their wives they will produce pure adamic offspring; from their negro concubines, they will produce mixed-bloods. The progeny of the latter, are always mixed-bloods, without reference to whether their mates are

WHAT IS A NIGGER

whites, mixed-bloods, or negroes.

While the absorbtion and destruction of the Negro, and the consequent increase of the mixed-bloods, is progressing, the Adamic females declining to lower themselves by association with their inferiors, the Negro and mixed-bloods, are confining their married relations to pure Adamic males; and are producing pure Adamic stock to very nearly the same extent as if there was no amalgamation going on between the Adamic males and the negroes and mixed-bloods. The mixed-blooded females, for obvious reasons, prefer the Adamic males, either in transient amours or as permanent mates. Under the influence of the law of heredity, the offspring resulting from these unhallowed unions, present more and more the physical and mental characters of the White, with each succeeding generation, until, in the course of time, it would never occur to the ordinary observer that they were not of pure Adamic stock. When this occurs, the mixed-blooded males, by a change of residence to a distant part

THE CASE OF THE CENTURIES

of the country, find it easy to impose themselves on the whites as pure-bloods, and are thus enabled to form marriage alliances with adamic females. When this lamentable result ensues, the Adamic Creation is successfully assaulted at its vital point-the female. The base-born products of God's violated law, resulting from these unions, will marry indiscriminately with pure whites. Then the doom of that nation is sealed. Nothing short of a direct intervention of Divine providence can save it.

When amalgamation begins in a nation, the relation of master and servant always exists between the whites and negroes. As this crime increases, no record is kept of the pure white, nor of the pure negroes, nor of the mixed-bloods. As in our own country, every individual whose skin is white, or relatively so, is recognized as pure white, unless he is known to be of negro extraction, or his antecedents are unknown. On the other hand, without reference to their complexion, all are recognized as negroes who are known to be tainted with negro blood. The

WHAT IS A NIGGER

result is, that at no time is it possible to discover that the mixed-bloods are rapidly increasing at the expense of both the pure whites and the pure negroes. Hence, each succeeding generation supposes that the conditions by which it is surrounded are such as always existed. In the meantime, God may visit his curses upon them in the form of war, famine, pestilence, etc., to compel them to abandon their crime and return to their allegiance to Him. Failing in this, God, in his wrath and disgust, may destory them from the face of the earth and lay their civilization in ruins. On the other hand, He may abandon them to the natural result of their shameless crime. In this case, as has been shown, the negroes will first be absorbed by their associations with the white males and the mixed-bloods. Then in their turn the whites will be absorbed through their associations with mixed-bloods. This accomplished, the relation of that nation to God and its relation to the earth and the rest of created things, has undergone the most radical change. Its original population of whites and negroes,

THE CASE OF THE CENTURIES

were parts of God's creation; while their amalgamated progeny is merely the product of His violated law. This change was so gradual, requiring many centuries for its completion, that it attracted no attention at the time. Hence, the cause which led to it is never investigated and understood. When the whites are finally destroyed, their country, with its civilization, wealth and national name, together with their religion, their knowledge of the arts, sciences, etc., is inherited by their mixed-blooded descendants. In many cases they are dispossessed of their civilization and driven into the forest where, with no capacity to develop a civilization for themselves, they descend to savagery. We find an illustration of this in the case of the Navajoes. At the time of the Spanish conquest, they were an agricultural community. Compelled by the Spaniards to abondon their inherited possessions, they sought shelter in the mountains. They never made the least effort to develop a civilization, but became a wandering band of as wild, blood-thirsty savages as ever infested the

WHAT IS A NIGGER

border, and are such today. (Baldwin's *Ancient America*.)

On the other hand, these mixed-bloods, in which the white blood largely predominates, may, under favorable conditions, retain more or less of their inherited possessions for an indefinite period. From among the numerous examples of this kind which are furnished by the various continents, we shall select Greece as an illustration, since her history, both ancient and modern, is more generally understood.

There was a period in the history of Greece when her people were famed throughout the world for their white skins, their fair hair and their possession of all the exalted physical and mental characters which are peculiar to that sublime creature whom God honored in the Creation by the bestowal of His "likeness" and His "image." In that remote age of her history, Greece gave to posterity a galaxy of intellects, whose names and whose achievements adorn the brightest pages in the world's history. But alas! alas! Their towering intellectuality, their

THE CASE OF THE CENTURIES

boundless enterprise, their restless energy, their dauntless courage, combined with their forgetfulness of God, paved the way to their ruin. During their various wars, thousands of negroes were captured and imported into Greece as slaves, together with thousands of captives taken from the mixed-blooded tribes and nations against which Greece waged war. These were never exported, yet they have long since disappeared, leaving no progeny of negroes in their stead. And it is a significant fact, and one which no anthropologist, no historian and no traveler will deny, that the white-skinned, fair-haired Greek of ancient times has also disappeared, leaving no progeny of white-skinned, fair-haired Greeks. What became of them? A glance at our surroundings should convince us that, in an evil hour, amalgamation laid its blighting touch upon the vitals of Greece; and, in the course of centuries, under its destructive influences, the white-skinned, fair-haired Greek and the black-skinned, woolly-haired Negro disappeared, and were replaced by

WHAT IS A NIGGER

the dark-skinned, black-haired Greek of modern times. This radical change in the physical characters of her population was accompanied by a corresponding change in their mentality, and, consequently, in the status of Greece among the nations of the earth; and that fair land, once the home of the highest culture, became the abode of ignorance and superstition. Many a long century has dragged its weary length into eternity since Greece produced a Homer, an Aristides, a Herodotus, a Pericles, a Solon, a Plato or a Demosthenes.

    Pausing amid the busy scenes of daily life to view the routes which man has trodden from the Creation to the Crucifixion, or even down to the fall of the Roman empire, or down to our day, if you will, we observe that, however divergent these routes may be in the ultimate, they all converge upon the Noachian Deluge. Scattered thickly along these various routes, we note the wrecks of principalities, kingdoms and empires, with here and there one which, in the zenith of its wealth and power, ruled the world. But alas!

THE CASE OF THE CENTURIES

Their glory has departed; their once intellectual, cultured and powerful populations no longer grace the earth-their name is history; in many instances even their national boundaries are stricken from the maps of the world; their once fertile fields, that bloomed and fruited in the smiles of heaven, and yeilded an abundant harvest as the reward of intelligent, industrious culture, are now barren wastes, which bear the unmistable impress of the curse of God and are properly described in Scripture as desolaions; their former cities, once the flourishing marts of the world's commerce, are now buried beneath the earth; or, if any vestige of them remains upon its surface still, a mass of ruins alone mark their sites; their once splendid capitals, within the palaces of which the royalty, the nobility, the intellect, the culture, the beauty, the chivalry, the wealth and fashion of those ancient realms held high revel, are now swept from the earth; or, if any vestige of them remains, they are in ruins and, like Petra, Idumea's once proud capital, they are degraded to fold for herds and flocks; or, like Nineveh,

WHAT IS A NIGGER

that city "that dwelt carelessly," they have "become a desolation; a place for beasts to lie down in;" or, like Palenque, the ruins of their former beauties and grandeurs are now buried in the gloom and solitude of the jungle. Their histories or their traditions, if any, have descended to us; or their monuments, or their inscriptions, if any remain, all teach us that, in their prosperous days, the White and the Black-Man and the Negro-were represented in their populations. But, strange as it may seem, it is nevertheless true, that any remnant of their descendants which can be identified, are colored-some shade of brown, red or yellow. If neither history, nor tradition, nor monument, nor inscription, nor remnant of their descendants can be found, an investigation of the ruins of their civilization reveals the idol-the most infallible evidence that amalgamation destroyed them.

THE CASE OF THE CENTURIES

Chapter VII.
That the Beast is Biped Animal, and not a Quadruped, is Proven by the Bible.

We observe that God treats the land animals, with which man was to be more closely associated on his efforts to "subdue" the earth, very differently from the manner in which he treats the "fowl of the air," or the "fish of the sea," in that he divides them into three classes, as shown by the following: "And God said, Let the earth bring forth the living creature after his kind, cattle, and creeping thing, and beast of the earth after his kind; and it was so." (Gen. i:24.) This division of the land animals into the three

WHAT IS A NIGGER

classes named, "cattle," "creeping things," and "beast" is observed throughout the scriptures.

Theologians who have noted this classification, and have attempted to interpret it, base the distinction which God makes between "cattle" and "beast" upon the nature of the food upon which they subsist; that is, they consider the "cattle" to be herbiverous animals; and the "beasts" to be carniverous animals. (See Guyot's *Creation*, Kinn's *Moses and Geology*, etc.). This interpretation not only brings the Narative of Creation in conflict with Bible history, as we shall hereafter show, but also brings it in conflict with the teachings of modern science. The first land animal to make its appearance on earth was a carniverous creature-an insect-eating marsupial. (Dana's *Manual of Geology*.) The distinction which God makes between "cattle" and "beast" is based upon the differences in their physical structure. The "cattle" are quadrupeds; the "beast" are bipeds-apes. Blumenbach, Cuvier and the older naturalists, regarded the apes as quadremana, or four-handed animals. But more

THE CASE OF THE CENTURIES

recent and careful investigation shows there is no four-handed animal. Prof. Huxley has shown, by comparative anatomy, that the fore, or upper extremity of every ape, from the Lemur up, is an arm, which terminates in a hand; and that the hinder or lower extremity of ever ape, from the Lemur up, is a leg, which terminates in a foot. (*Man's Place in Nature*.) Hence, the apes, like man, are bipeds. Our interpretation of God's division of the land animals, into three classes named, harmonizes with the teachings of modern science. Geological researches show that these three classes of creatures made their appearance on the earth, in the order stated in the Narrative of Creation: (1) Marsupials-quadrupeds (cattle). (2) A variety of animal forms, consisting of insects, worms snakes, etc. (creeping things). (3) apes-bipeds (beasts). [See Dana's *Manual of Geology*.]

Inasmuch as the physical and mental organisms of the ape are in nearer approach to those of man, than are those of the quadrupeds, it follws that he is a higher grade of animal.

WHAT IS A NIGGER

Hence, while the "cattle" and the whole of the land animals are sometimes referred to in scripture as "beasts," this higher grade of animal, the "beast," is never referred to in the Bible as "cattle." The quadrupeds are frequently refered to in the Bible as "cattle," "herds," or "flocks," and individual species of quadripeds, or "cattle," are frequently referred to as the horse, ox, swine, dog, lion, etc. On the other hand, the ape is specially named, or referred to as "beasts;" but never as "cattle," or "herbs," or "flocks." The careful observance of this unvarying rule will prove invaluable in our search of the scriptures. We must carefully observe the distinction which God makes between the "cattle," or quadrupeds, and "beast," or ape.

We observe that, in addition to commanding the earth to "bring forth cattle and creeping things," God commanded it to bring forth the beast of the earth after his kind; that is, after the beast or ape kind. Theologians pay no attention to this command, supposing it to be a general term, which is applied to the carniverous

THE CASE OF THE CENTURIES

animals. This is a mistake; it is the name which God applied to a particular ape, as shown by the following:

"And the fear of you and the dread of you shall be upon every beast of the earth and upon every fowl of the air, upon all that moveth upon the earth, and upon all the fishes of the sea; into your hand are they delivered." [Gen. ix.:2.] God thus names (1) the beast of the earth, (2) the fowl of the air, (3) "all that moveth upon the earth," [4] the fish of the sea. Thus we see that in this statement, the "beast of the earth" is separated from the rest of the land animals by the "fowl of the air." Thus it is shown that the term "beast of the earth," is not a general term applied to the carnivora, but is the name of a particular race of the "beast," or ape species. The importance and value of the "beast of the earth," in the execution of God's plan for the development of the resources of the earth, is indicated by the fact that he is the only animal specifically named in the Creation. No special mention is made of the horse, ox, etc. They are merely included with

WHAT IS A NIGGER

the rest of the quadrupeds under the general term cattle. In this respect he is on a par with man.

Bearing in mind the distinction which God makes between the "cattle," or quadrupeds, and the "beast," or ape, the following, in common with other punishments which God said he would inflict upon the Israelites if they violated His law, is significant: "And thy carcass shall be meat unto all fowls of the air and unto the beasts of the earth, and no man shall fray them away." [Deut. xxviii.:26.]

Then, said David to the Philistine, "This day will the Lord deliver thee into my hand. * * * And I will give the carcasses of the host of the Philistines this day unto the fowls of the air, and to the wild beasts of the earth." [I Sam. xvii.:45-46.]

This indicated that there were "wild beasts of the earth" in that region in that day. They had doubtless been emancipated. And it is significant that every one of the great nations of the region, with the exception of a scattered remnant of the Israelites, are destroyed from off the earth and

THE CASE OF THE CENTURIES

their civilizations are in ruins. Later on we shall have occasion to refer to the Philistine's challenge to David, with its accompanying threat. Thus, the Bible plainly teaches that there is a "beast," or ape, that is man eater. Yet, not one of the recognized apes of to-day, are man eaters. What became of this great man-eating ape? When we appeal to science to solve this problem, she promptly invades the so-called "human species," and points us to the Negro as the highest grade of ape, and the only ape that is a man eater. The Negro is not only a man eater, but he feeds upon the flesh of his own kindred, and even upon his own offspring, as well as upon that of other apes. Though the Negro made his appearance upon earth as the "beast of the earth," and is sometimes referred to by that name, it is not the only name, nor the one most frequently applied to him in scripture. This was simply the name which God applied to the Negro previous to the creation of man. The task of naming the animals developed upon Adam. We are taught that, "Adam gave names to all catttle, and to the fowl of the air, and

WHAT IS A NIGGER

to every beast of the field," [Gen. ii.:20.] Observe the distinction made between the "cattle" and the "beast of the field:" and that, in this statement, the fowl are placed between the "cattle" and the "beast of the field." Theologians pay little or no attention to the "beast of the field," and seem to take it for granted that the "beast of the field" are that class of animals which were designed to be harnessed to the beam and draw the plow. But a careful investigation of this subject reveals the startling truth that this was the creature whom God designed should grasp the handles and direct the team.

When we approach the modern Christian, either priest or layman, with the inquiry, "What is the 'beast of the field?'" he promptly replies: "These are our domestic animals of draught and burthen, the horse, the ox, and the ass, with which we cultivate the fields, and use for other domestic purposes." As is well known, our domestic animals of draught and burthen with which we cultivate the fields, subsist on grass, hay and the cereals; not one of them is a flesh

THE CASE OF THE CENTURIES

eating animals. But the bibical "beast of the field is a flesh eating creature; he is the worst form of flesh eating animal; he is a man eater, as shown by the following: "And the Philistine said to David, Come to me and I will give thy flesh unto the fowls of the air, and to the beast of the field." [I Sam. xvii.:44.] Among the "cattle," or quadrupeds, are numerous carniverous animals that will feed upon the flesh of man; but, as has been shown, the Negro is the only "beast," or ape that will feed upon the flesh of man. Hence, the "beast of the field" to which the Philistine said he would give the flesh of David, and the "beast of the earth" to which David said he would give the flesh of the Philistine were identical. This indicates (1) that when Adam named the animals, he named the Negro the "beast of the field;" (2) that both the Philistines and the Israelites recognized the Negro as a beast. The negro made his appearance upon the earth as the "beast of the earth" and is sometimes referred to by that name. When Adam named the animals he named the Negro "the beast of the field;" and this name

WHAT IS A NIGGER

is generally applied to him in scripture, though he is frequently referred to simply as "beast."

Further evidence that the "beast of the field" is a man eater, is furnished by Rizpah's touching exhibition of mother love and devotion in guarding the bodies of her sons who were hanged by David's order. Rizpah "took sackcloth and spread it for her upon the rock from the beginning of harvest until water dropped upon them our of heaven, and suffered neither the birds of the air to rest upon them by day, nor the beasts of the field by night." (II. Sam xxi.:10.)

Further evidence of the broad distinction which God makes between the "cattle" and the "beast," is shown in the narrative of the plagues with which God afflicted the Egyptians, to compel them to let Isreal go. After afflicting them with frogs, lice, flies, etc., God said to Moses, "Go unto Pharaoh, and tell him, Behold, the hand of the Lord is upon thy cattle, which is in the field, upon the horses, upon the asses, upon the camels, upon the oxen, and upon the sheep; there shall be a very grievous murrian. And the Lord shall

THE CASE OF THE CENTURIES

sever between the cattle of Isreal and the cattle of Egypt; and there shall nothing die of all that is the children's of Israel. And the Lord did that thing on the morrow, and all the cattle of Egypt died; but of the cattle of the children of Israel died not one. And the heart of pharoah was hardened, and he did not let the people go. And the Lord said unto Aaron, Take to you handfuls of ashes of the furnace, and let Moses sprinkle it toward the heaven in the sight of Pharoah. And it shall become small dust in all the land of Egypt, and shall be boil breaking forth with blains upon man and upon beast, throughout all the land of Egypt. And they took the ashes of the furances, and stood before Pharaoh; and Moses sprinkled it toward heaven; and it became a boil breaking forth with blains upon man and upon beast." (Ex. ix, i, 3, 4, etc.)

We are thus taught (1) that the "cattle" are quadrupeds, horses, camels, etc. And that the "beasts" were a very different class of animals, as shown by the fact that the "cattle" were first afflicted; then afterwards the "beasts" were

WHAT IS A NIGGER

afflicted. This is signigcant, when we consider that each succeeding plague was more injurious to the Egyptians than its predecessor. This indicates the relative value of the "cattle" and "beasts," and that the "beasts" were far more valuable than the "cattle." We can readily understand that this would be so, when we realize that the "cattle" were their domestic quadrupeds, and that their "beasts" were negroes. Previous to the late sectional war in the United States, the negroes in the Southern States were far more valuable than the domestic quadrupeds in those States. A sheep was worth say $2.00; a cow or an ox $25.00; a horse $100.00. But an adult negro was worth from $1,000.00 to $1,500.00. Hence, it was far more injurious to the people of the South to be deprived of their negroes than it would have been to deprive them of their domestic quadrupeds. The same was doubtless true of the Egyptains of Pharaoh's day. Profane history and science teach that the Egyptians owned immense numbers of negroes. The negro is figured on the Egyptian monuments of 4,000 years ago. (2)

THE CASE OF THE CENTURIES

The "cattle" of Egyptians were afflicted with "a very grievous murrain," while the "beasts" were afflicted with "boils breaking forth into blains," just as the men of Egypt were. This is significant. (3) the Egyptians, who were masters of the country, are accredited with owning both "cattle" and "beasts," while the Isrealites, who were in bondage to the Egyptians, are accredited with owning "cattle" but not "beasts." (See Ex. x, 9, 24, 25; Ex. xii, 38.)

The Canaanites, whom the Israelites were commanded to destroy, and possess themselves of their country, were the owners of great numbers of negroes, as shown by the following; "And the Lord thy God will put out those nations before thee by little and by little; thou mayest not consume them at once, lest the beasts of the field increase upon thee." (Deut. vii, 22.) Observe that there was no fear expressed lest the "cattle" or the "creeping thing" increase upon the Israelites! But not so with the "beasts of the field"- the negroes. Let us bear in mind that the country of the Canaanites was a rich, productive

WHAT IS A NIGGER

country, "a goodly land;" and that it was in the highest state of cultivation-"a land flowing with milk and honey;" that it abounded with cities, towns, villages, farms, vineyards, orchards, etc. And that it was ocupied by "seven nations greater and mightier" than Israel. And it would have been impossible for this comparatively small number of Israelites to have occupied the numerous fine cities, towns, villages, farms, etc., and maintain this splendid civilization which had required ages to develop. It was the expressed desire of God that the land of Canaan, with its wealth of every description, should become the property of the Israelites; and if the Canaanites were all destroyed "at once," much of their civilization would crumble into ruins for the want of being cared for; and it would require centuries for the Israelites to increase to such an extent as would enable them to occupy the entire land. Hence, it was the part of wisdom for the Israelites to first possess themselves of only so much of the land as they could successfully handle; leaving the remainder with

THE CASE OF THE CENTURIES

its wealth and civilization in the hands of the Canaanites to care for and preserve. In addition to this, it seems that there was a greater number of negroes in the land of Canaan than the Israelites could at first profitably handle; so if the canaanites were all destroyed at once, much of the civilization and wealth of these seven nations would fall into the hands of the negroes and be wasted and destroyed. The negro is as prolific as the white, and would increase as rapidly; they would prove very troublesome neighbors; as the freed negro never fails to prove. Besides, it would have been a violation of the law of God to release the negro form the control of their former owners and give them no new ones. Hence, "The Lord thy God will put these nations out before thee by little and by little; thou mayest not consume them at once, lest the beasts of the filed increase upon thee."

The evidence that the Israelites possessed negroes is found in the following command: "And six years shalt thou sow thy land, and shalt let it rest and lie still; that the poor of thy people

WHAT IS A NIGGER

may eat; and what they leave the beasts of the field shall eat. In like manner thou shalt deal with thy vineyard, and with thy olive yard." (Ex. xxiii, 10, 11.)

Here we have additional and positive proof that the "beast of the field" is not our domestic quadrupeds of draught and buthen; these animals will not eat grapes and olives. Besides, it is not supposable that God would require the Isralites to turn their oxen, horses, etc., into their vineyards and olive yards to browse, trample down, and destroy them every seventh year. The negro would gather the grapes and olives and not injure the vineyard or olive yards. Besides, the negro will eat the products of the fields, gardens, orchards and vineyards, or anything that a man will eat, and then eat the man. God's love and wisdom is displayed in this command restraining the Israelites from á abandoning themselves to a mad, ceaseless struggle for the accumulation of wealth. Every seventh year the land was not to be cultivated; it should "rest and lie still;" and any spontaneous crops which it might produce

THE CASE OF THE CENTURIES

should be for the poor people; and what they left should be for the negroes. The latter were cared for by their masters, so that they could dispose of their part, and thus realize more or less cash for their own use. So it was with the vineyards and olive yards. These would, of course, produce as abundantly as in any other year. The land-owners were allowed to reserve such parts of the crops of these as were necessary for their own use, but the surplus was not to be sold; this should belong to the poor people, and what they left should be for the negroes. Thus, under God's wise, beneficent law, all were cared for- the land-owners, the poor and the negroes. Thus, the negroes were not compelled to labor incessantly, year after year, without compensation; but in addition to such "tips" as they might receive from time to time, they were allowed to share in the products of the land every seventh year.

The following charge of the Almighty is one of the many with which the Scriptures abound, which go to prove that the Israelites

WHAT IS A NIGGER

violated the law of God and descended to amalgamation with the negroes and with the mixed-bloods: "For mine eyes are upon all their ways. * * * And first I will recompense their iniquity and their sin double; because they have defiled my land, they have filled mine inheritance with the carcasses of their detestable and abominable things." (Jer. xvi, 17, 18.) Thus, the Israelites, like the antedeluvians and the Canaanites, defiled the land. What is God's "inheritance?" Israel was God's inheritance. (See I. Kings viii, 51; Isaiah xix, 25, etc.) Then, by their amalgamation, they had defiled the land and had "filled" Israel-the nation of Israel-with the "carcasses" of "things" that were "detestable and abominable" in the sight of God. Observe that in producing those "detestable and abominable things" they had defiled the land, just as the Canaanites had done. Observe also that the Creator of the heaven and the earth, the Maker of man and beast, He who fashioned the fowl of the air and the fish of the sea-God, the Author of all language and all speech-declined

THE CASE OF THE CENTURIES

to give a name to this loathsome offspring of Man and the Negro; and the nearest approach that he would make to naming them is found in his declination recorded in our text, when, in the absence of all name (for these monstrosities are nameless) he bestows upon them the descriptive epithet, "detestable and abominable things."

The above text throws a flood of light upon God's command to Jeremiah: "Thou shalt not take thee a wife, neither shalt thou have sons or daughters in this place. For this saith the Lord concerning the sons and concerning the daughters that are born in this place, and concerning their mothers that bare them, and concerning their fathers that begat them in this land: They shall die grievous deaths; they shall not be lamented, neither shall they be buried; but they shall be as dung upon the face of the earth; and they shall be consumed by the sword, and by famine; and their carcasses shall be meat for the fowl of heaven and for the beasts of the earth." (Jer. xvi, 2, 3.)

We are thus taught: (1) That the men of Israel had persisted in amalgamation so long that

WHAT IS A NIGGER

their male progeny of mixed-bloods were not distinguishable from pure whites; and that in this way many of the women of Israel had been led into amalgamation. Hence, it was dangerous for a man to take a wife from among them, and Jeremiah was forbidden to do so.

(2) That, in the eyes of God, the offspring of Man and the Negro is only fit for dung on the face of the earth.

It will be observed that the Bible describes two offenses which result from illicit intercourse between the sexes. The one is termed "adultery," the other "fornication." The modern world has been taught to believe that "adultery" is "the unfaithfulness of any married person to the marriage bed." (Webster, *Dictionary*.) And that "fornication" is "the incontinence or lewdness of unmarried persons, male or female." [*Ibid.*] This is opposed to the teachings of scripture. Our Saviour said, "It hath been said, whosoever shall put away his wife, saving for the cause of fornication, causes her to commit adultery; and whosoever shall marry her committeth adultery."

THE CASE OF THE CENTURIES

(Matt. xix, 9.) Here we observe the distinction made between fornication and adultery; and that a married person may commit fornicaiton. But if for any other cause save fornication a man put away his wife, and another man marries her, both the woman and the man whom she marries commit adultery, but not fornication.

As has been shown, Cain, and other antediluvias, and the people of Sodom and Gomorrha, and the Israelites, were all charged by Jude with committing fornication and "going after strange flesh." Adultery is that offense which men and women commit by illicit intercourse with their own kind of flesh. But fornication is that offense which men and women commit when they associate themselves carnally with the negro, or with mixed-bloods; that is, with strange flesh. The New Testament abounds with denunciations of fornication and fornicators, which indicate that fornication was prevalent in the days of the Savior; and that, like the prophets who preceded him, his mission was to break up this wicked, destructive practice, and the social,

WHAT IS A NIGGER

political and religious equality with the negro which inevitably leads to it; and to restore the relation of master and servant which God established between man and negro in the creation.

God charges that the people of Jerusalem and Samaria committed fornication with the Egyptians, Assyrians, etc., whose "flesh is as the flesh of asses, and whose issue is as the issue of horses." (Ezek. xxiii, 20.) When we turn upon this statement the light of Paul's declaration that "there is one kind of flesh of men, another flesh of beasts," etc., it becomes plain that the horse and the ass and the negro all belong to one kind of flesh-the flesh of beasts; and that Egyptians, Assyrians, etc., had descended to amalgamation. Hence, their flesh was corrupted, and was strange flesh to that of the people of Jerusalem and Samaria. Bearing this in mind, the following is instructive:

"Son of man, set thy face against Pharaoh, king of Egypt, and prophesy against him, and against all Egypt. * * * Therefore thus saith the

THE CASE OF THE CENTURIES

Lord God: Behold, I will bring a sword upon thee, and cut off man and beast out of thee. And the land of Egypt shall be desolate and waste. No foot of man shall pass through it, nor foot of beast shall pass through it neither shall it be inhabited forty years. And I will make the land of Egypt desolate in the midst of the countries that are desolate, and her cities among the cities that are laid waste, shall be desolate forty years; and I will scatter the Egyptians among the nations, and will disperse them through the countries. Yet thus saith the Lord God: At the end of forty years will I gather the Egyptians whither they were scattered. And I will bring again the captivity of Egypt, and will cause them to return into the land of Pathros, into the land of their habitation; and they shall become a base kingdom. * * * Therefore thus saith the Lord God: Behold, I will give the land of Egypt unto Nebuchadrezzar, king of Babylon; and he shall take her multitude, and take her spoil, and take her prey; and it shall be the wages of his army." [Ezek. xxix, 2, 8, 9, etc.]

WHAT IS A NIGGER

Thus, we are plainly taught by the Bible that, acting under Divine influence, Nebuchadrezzar invaded Egypt and took the Egyptians captive, and scattered them through the countries over which Babylon held sway; and that neither foot of man nor foot of beast passed through Egypt for forty years; that the land of Egypt was utterly waste and desolate, and was not inhabited for forty years. In direct conflict with this Bible teaching, profane history, sustained by scientific research, teaches that from the first settlement after the deluge Egypt has always been inhabited in the sense that we understand the term.

Now, if we accept the teachings of atheism and those of the modern church that the whites, blacks, browns, reds and yellows are all "races of men" in different stages of development, how are we to reconcile the teachings of profane history and of science with the Bible, as to this forty years of Egyptian history? Shall we decide that Nebuchadrezzar entered Egypt and carried away every white, black, brown, red and yellow

THE CASE OF THE CENTURIES

of the so-called "races of men," and that in addition to this he removed every animal, wild and tame, great and small, and thus left Egypt "utterly waste and desolate," and that she remained in this condition forty years? This would be absurd. But when we disabuse our minds of this atheistic theory that man is a "species" which is divisible into "races of men," and accept the teachings of scripture and the sciences that the white is the only man, and that the negro is an ape, and that the reds, browns and yellows are the result of amalgamation between whites and negroes, and are not a part of God's creation, this subject becomes plain. We can understand that Nebuchadrezzar entered Egypt and removed every pure-blooded white and every pure-blooded negro, leaving the lower animals and the mixed-bloods; and that God declined to recognize these base-born products of his violated law as inhabitants. And that neither "the foot of man" nor "the foot" of beast (negro) passed through Egypt for forty years. When the whites were all removed, and the mixed-bloods left,

WHAT IS A NIGGER

then, in the eyes of God Egypt was "waste and desolate" and was not "inhabited," and so remained for forty years. This shows that a country which is occupied solely by mixed-bloods is in the eyes of God "waste and desolate" and not "inhabited." Yet the modern church is expending millions of dollars annually in the vain, criminal effort to Christianize these degraded creatures which God has declared to be only fit for dung on the face of the earth.

    The attitude of the modern clergy toward the negro is in striking contrast to that of David, who, in discussing God's creation of man, says: "Thou madest him to have dominion over the works of thy hands; thou has put all things under his feet. All sheep and oxen, yea, and the beasts of the field." (Ps. viii, 6, 7.) David realized that he had no "brother in black;" on the contrary, he recognized the negro as a beast, "the beast of the field." But then David also realized that man was a distinct creation "in the image of God" and that he was not a highly developed species of ape-the "human species"-of which the White is

THE CASE OF THE CENTURIES

the highest and the Negro the lowest race. This, of course, would explain the difference.

Further evidence that our views as to the characters peculiar to man must be materially modified is shown by the narrative of the Fall, as follows:

"Now the serpent was more subtle than any beast of the field which the Lord God had made. And he said to the woman, Yea, hath God said, Ye shall not eat of every tree of the garden? And the woman said unto the serpent, We may eat of the fruit of the trees of the garden, but of the fruit of the tree which is in the midst of the garden God hath said, Ye shall noteat of it, neither shall ye touch it lest ye die. And the serpent said unto the woman, Ye shall not surely die: For God doth know that in the day ye eat thereof, then your eyes shall be opened and ye shall be as gods, knowing good and evil. And when the woman saw that the tree was good for food, and that it was pleasant to the eyes, and a tree to be desired to make one wise, she took of the fruit thereof, and did eat, and gave also unto

WHAT IS A NIGGER

her husband with her and he did eat. And the eyes of them both were opened, and they knew that they were naked, and they sewed fig leaves together and made themselves aprons. And they heard the voice of the Lord God walking in the garden in the cool of the day. And Adam and his wife hid themselves from the presence of the Lord God amongst the trees of the garden. And the Lord God called unto Adam and said unto him, Where art thou? And he said, I heard thy voice in the garden and I was afraid because I was naked, and I hid myself. And he said, Who told thee that thou was naked? Hast thou eaten of the tree whereof I commanded thee thou shouldst not eat? And the man said, The woman thou gavest to be with me, she gave me of the tree, and I did eat. And the Lord God said unto the woman, What is this that thou hast done? And the woman said, The serpent beguiled me and I did eat. And the Lord said unto the serpent, Because thou hast done this thou art cursed above all cattle and above every beast of the field; upon thy belly shalt thou go, and dust shalt

THE CASE OF THE CENTURIES

thou eat all the days of thy life." (Gen. iii.)

We observe (1) that the tempter of Eve was a beast of the field. This would scarely have been more clearly indicated had the text read, "Now the serpent was more subtle than any other beast of the field which the Lord God had made." (2) It is evident that when Adam gave names "to every beast of the field" with which he was to be associated in the garden of Eden, in his efforts "to dress it and to keep it," the characteristics displayed by this individual led Adam to name it the serpent. This was simply a name given it to distiuguish it from others of its kind. Hence, the name Serpent no more indicated that it was a snake than does the name of the late Indian chief, Sitting Bull, indicate that he was a bull which habitually assumed the sitting posture. (3) Observe the adroitness with which this beast approached Eve with the inquiry, "Yea, hath God said, Ye shall not eat of every tree in the garden?" The language employed clearly indicated that this creature was perfectly familiar with the subject of which, in pretended ignorance,

WHAT IS A NIGGER

he was seeking information. And when viewed in the light of subsequent events, it becomes plain that this question was a part of a well-conceived and skillfully-executed plan to deceive the woman into violating the law of God. Just here Eve made the mistake of her life; she should have rebuked this creature and sent him about his business. But instead of doing this the unsuspecting woman in the simplicity of her nature frankly replied: "we may eat of the fruits of the garden. But of the fruit of the tree which is in the midst of the garden, God hath said, Ye shall not eat of it, neither shall ye touch it lest ye die."

"And the serpent said unto the woman, Ye shall not surely die. For God doth know that in the day ye eat thereof, then your eyes shall be opened, and ye shall be as gods, knowing good and evil." Then, emboldened by his success in gaining the confidence of the woman, the serpent proceeds (1) to assail the word of God; (2) to instil into the woman's heart distrust of God; [3] to engender in her mind discontent with her lot;

THE CASE OF THE CENTURIES

[4] to arouse in her the unhallowed ambition that she and her husband "be as gods." As shown by the narrative, the serpent accomplished his iniquitous design. The woman, accompanied by Adam, and perhaps by the serpent, approached the forbidden tree, and "took of the fruit thereof, and did eat and gave also unto her husband with her, and he did eat."

The modern clergy teach that the first sin which Adam and Eve committed was their eating of the forbidden fruit. This, as shown by the record, is in direct conflict with the plain teaching of the Bible. When they accepted as their councilor this creature over which they were designed to "have dominion," they violated those original statutes given man in the creation, and thus brought sin into the world. Instead of controlling this "beast of the field," or negro-the serpent-they allowed him to control them, and he led them to their ruin. Their acceptance of this beast as their councilor necessarily preceded their acting upon his advice. Hence, their eating of the forbidden fruit was a second and later

WHAT IS A NIGGER

offense. This reveals the startling fact that it was man's social equality with the negro which brought sin into the world; and it is man's social equality with the negro and the evils which inevitably grows out of it that keeps sin in the world.

We observe that the first curses which God visited upon the serpent were directed solely at his posture. Had the tempter of Eve been a snake, God's sentence, "Upon thy belly shalt thou go," would have been of no effect; it would not have wrought the slightest change in the posture of the snake; neither would it have occasioned him the least inconvenience. On the other hand, it would have placed God in the most ridiculous light, since the only way the snake could go was upon his belly. But when we come to understand that the tempter of Eve was a beast-a negro-this whole subject appears in a very different light. The habitual posture of the negro is the erect. Hence, God's sentence, "Upon thy belly shalt thou go," wrought the most terrible

THE CASE OF THE CENTURIES

punishment. When God cursed him "above every beast of the field," it deprived him of his erect posture. When God cursd him "above all cattle," he was prevented from going upon all fours, like the quadrupeds. "Upon thy belly shalt thou go" degraded him, in point of posture, to the level of the lowest of the "creeping things."

God's other curse upon the serpent, "I will put enmity between thee and the woman, and between thy seed and her seed; it shall bruise thy head, and thou shalt bruise his heel," shows that the tempter of Eve was a material creature; a creature of flesh and blood: and that he begat offspring. And it is highly probable that he was the parent of Cain's paramour of strange flesh; and that this curse was fulfilled in Cain's ultimate banishment from the Adamic family to become, "a fugitive and vagabond in the earth," and an outcast in eternity.

It should be unnecessary to state that God's curses upon the tempter of Eve were confined to this offending beast, and did not extend to the rest of the negroes, since they were

WHAT IS A NIGGER

not parties to his crime.

We also observe that this "beast of the field" which tempted Eve possessed articulate speech; and that his mental capacity was such as enabled him to fully understand Adam's relations to the Garden of Eden and its plants, and the laws governing his conduct. And that he was sufficiently subtle to deceive man into violating the laws of God.

Thus, the Bible describes (1) a beast whose habitual posture is the erect; this necessitates a well-formed leg and foot; (2) a beast with a hand. God said of the mountain at Sinai, "There shall not a hand touch it * * * whether it be beast or man." (Ex. xix, 13;) (3) a beast with articulate speech; (4) a beast with mental capacity sufficient to enable him to understand the laws of God, and to deceive man into violating them, (5) a beast with which man may associate himself carnally and produce offspring which will at once be indefinitely fertile and capable of appreciating and utilizing all the arts of civilization.

It seems plain that in addition to his

THE CASE OF THE CENTURIES

general plan of salvation God devised a great labor plan for development of the resources of the earth. That the execution of this plan was entrusted to man, who was designed to perform the mental labor. That the beasts or apes should furnish in the negro the creature which, in the capacity of servant, should perform the manual labor. And that the "cattle" or quadrupeds should furnish the animals of draught and burthen; and together with the fish and fowl, would furnish man and the negro their supply of animal food.

The Bible is simply a history of the long conflict which has raged between God and man, as the result of man's criminal relations with the negro. Hence, when we recognize the negro as a man, we can make no more sense out of the Bible than we could make out of the history of the American Revolution and recognize the Tories as a part of Washington's army. But when we accept the teachings of scripture that man is a distinct creation "in the image of God;" and that the negro is an ape; and that man's criminal relations with the negro have been the prolific

WHAT IS A NIGGER

source of all the trouble between God and man since the Creation, the mystery with which atheism has enveloped the Bible disappears; and that sublime current of inspired truth-the Sacred Narrative-from Genesis to Revelations glides as smoothly as a stream of oil; not the slightest ripple of discord mars its majestic flow.

Already science has sounded the note of warning. M. Reclus, and M. L'abbe de Bonbourg, quoted by Quatrefages, says that "at the end of a given time, whatever be their origin, all the descendants of whites or of negroes who have emigrated to America will become redskins." (The Human Species.) What is the redskin? Simply a savage. Then under the leadership of Enlightened Christianity, and modern Materialism, with their miserable theory that man is a "species which is divisible into races," we are descending to savagery; to ruin in time, and to hades in eternity. While we agree with the distinguished authors above quoted that the whites and the blacks will disappear from America, we do not agree with them that their

THE CASE OF THE CENTURIES

descendants will all become redskins. We admit that redskins will be found here and there; but, in tribes where the blood of the white largely predomintes, we shall have our Maudans, Decotas, Tuscaroras, Zunians, Menominees, etc. In other tribes, where the blood of the negro largely predominates, we shall have our Kaws, Carabees, Charuas, Jamassi, etc. When, through the factional strifes of our mixed-blooded descendants, our government is broken up into so many hostile tribes, as was that of our ancient predecessors, the marriage relations of each will be confined to their own tribe. The white and black blood will be equally distributed to every member of it; their physical and mental characters will be in the course of time become fixed. Our descendants will then present every shade of complexion intermediate between that of the pure White and that of the pure Negro.

The negro, like man, made his appearance upon the earth without weapons either offensive or defensive. But soon realizing the necessity for weapons, his mechanical skill, an essential

WHAT IS A NIGGER

of stone. These chipped flints are the earlist evidences of art to be found on the globe. They abound in what is termed the Paleolithic, or Age of Rough Stone. Man was created a metalurgist. How could man subdue the earth without a knowledge of metal? The mixed bloods, who had lost their knowledge of metals, were the artisans of the finely-wrought and polished implements of the Molithic or Age of Polished Stone. Quatrefages compares the so-called "Cromagnon Race" of Europe to the Algonquin Indian. *(The Human Species)*.

CLOSING:

You, reader(s), are the juror(s). You have heard (read) the case of the Centuries under the title "Mommie, What is a Nigger?" The case has been presented to you by the plaintiffs. Keep in mind that the defendants never had access to the plaintiff's so-called "convincing evidence" against the defendants. Also, the plaintiffs have stated in their own words that they have applied and taught much of their "convincing evidence" to others within their group.

Throughout this entire case the plaintiffs vowed that they would give evidence to prove what the Negro - is. The plaintiffs started out by giving you information on the "formation of the Negro - "biblical and scientific facts that the Negro - is not of Adam's family, not of the human family. (Caucasians) The Negro is soulless; the red, yellow and brown skin comes from the amalgamation of the human family (Caucasians) with the Negro. What does the Bible say? (Genesis chapter 1, 2, 3 & 4, Psalms, 139: 1-24)

In the end, the plaintiffs state that they

were justified in having negroes as slaves. "As a matter of fact, the Negro was never a slave. To conceive the design of enslaving an individual we must presuppose that he is free; the first act of enslavement is to deprive him of his liberty. This the Negro never had since the creation of man. The Negro is an ape; hence, his status in the universe, his relation to man, like that of every other animal, was fixed irrevocably by God in the creation, and no act upon man's part, whether legislative, executive or judicial, can change it. The will of God upon this most important subject, as expressed in those original statutes given man in the creation, Have dominion over the fish of the sea, and over the fowl of the air, and over every living thing that moveth upon the earth, is the supreme law of the universe; and in the eyes of this great law there is not today, there never was and there can never be on this earth, such a thing as a free Negro".

"God devise (sic) a great labor plan for the development of the resources of the earth. That the execution of this plan was entrusted to man (white), who was designed to perform the mental labor. That the beast or apes should furnish in the negro - the creature which, in the capacity, of servant, should perform the manual labor."

"The negro lack (sic) the spiritual creation which forms the link of kinship between God and man . . . , and The history of every nationality of ancient time, sustained by our experience with the negro in the United States, demonstrates that the White must be master of the negro, else they can never live together in peace."

Therefore, we believe the "nigger word" originated from the plaintiffs' so-called "convincing evidence," and we ask you (reader), the juror(s) to bring this case before the Almighty Judge since the plaintiffs categorically implicate the Almighty Judge as the Creator of the negro - (*negroid, negress, nigger, colored and black.*) All of these words at one time or another were applied to Africans and African Americans. The Almighty Judge will render the verdict and the sentence in due time.

" . . . What is a Nigger, The Case of the Centuries? We could only show you from the plaintiffs side. We have no earthly idea as to What Is a Nigger? This research has revealed, and we hope you have gained some long overdue knowledge presented by the plaintiffs against the African American group which we know have been called *negro, negroid, negress, nigger, colored and black*. The juror(s) must decide also whether any in the plaintiff group has injected their so-called "convincing evidence" into Bible teachings; the systematic break down of families (African Americans in particular); economics (joblessness, poor housing, poverty); social inequality (incarceration, drugs, alcohol); inequality of educational opportunity; and the government (federal, state, city and county).

The nigger word and what has been built on it negatively must be placed on the table and discussed openly. Our children must not fight racism on the level of the "nigger word", and what some have been taught against another group within the human family. This should have been buried four hundred years ago, in fact, it should not have ever happened. To literally destroy people mainly because one wants to be superior is the first and foremost violent act that America or any nation has ever perpetuated.

We did not research the "nigger word" because the word or the use of the word bothers or offends us. Years of researching this word and the background of it revealed that the "nigger word" is a European word. There is no country called *negro, negroid, negress, nigger, coon, colored, or black.* Just the opposite. We researched and released these portions on the bases of *Mommie, What is a Nigger* because of the open use of the word by some European Americans in the last seconds of this century, and our son asked us this question. We feel that if our child is thinking and asking such questions, there are millions of other alert children thinking and asking the same. We researched this to help parents and other young people (especially African Americans) not to fall prey to anyone of the European ethnic group, or any other who might call them "nigger", and African Americans responding to this by getting into a confrontation, which almost always leads into jail, or something negative. Having knowledge of what some of them mean when they say such would give African Americans a mental weapon that would destroy the "nigger word" along with the meanings and the institutions that fostered those beliefs about the African Americans.

We knew we could not go to another African American and get the answers to this question. The answer to this question could only come from some out of the Caucasian group, because the word and its foundation was born from this group. The meaning of this word was coined by some from this group. The structures based upon the meaning(s) of this word came out of some from this group, and became law for the others that were taught such.

There are three systems in which this group structured the meaning for the "nigger word". These three systems are (1) religion/education (some Africans, African Americans were forbidden to learn how to read anything), (2) family (some systematic break down of the family - Africans, African Americans in particular 1500 - 1995), and (3) the government (denying African Americans positions to serve the federal, state, city and county governments).

We are also concerned about the use of the word so openly and loosely by some within the Caucasian group over the past decade. Since history has shown that some whites have used their authority to produce the "nigger", what does the use of the word mean to them today? The accounts that are listed in my introduction are just a few. But, what amazes us more is that the majority of those that are in these accounts are young and they were taught through the supposedly "integrated school" systems. This system of teaching (niggerology) is so deep within some that they will murder their wife, unborn child or their children, then accuse a "black male", (African American) of doing such. This system will take a poll to prove which murder is worse.

To those within the African American group we want you to re-read this research carefully. African Americans who feel a need to use this word for the lack of a better word, you might want to really address their male friends as "brothers", and female friends as "sisters".

It is hoped that you have picked up in this reading what many of us have picked up. What is this? The writer of this old book said that God created the negro (*negress, negroid, nigger, colored and black*) as a beast, and Cain went out and had sexual relationship with one of the female beasts. The Amalgamation of these sexual contacts produced in essence "niggers". So, when you use the word even in a friendly gesture, you are reinforcing the teachings and the negative spirits based upon this word toward you, your mother, father, children and the African and African American group within the human family.

The writer of the old book also states in Chapter 4 that the marriage arrangement was performed upon the human being (white); therefore spiritual contact can only be between the humans (Adams, Eve and all offsprings from this pure lineage - white) and the Almighty God. God did not perform a marriage between Cain and his female "Negress"; therefore, all Africans and African Americans are soulless. They were not created to be in a marriage, but to reproduce for the purpose of the "great labor plan for the development of the resources of the earth. The execution of this plan was entrusted to man (white), who was designed to perform the mental labor . . . . . " Are you fathering and birthing children on this earth outside of the marriage arrangement, not giving them their fathers' last name, not loving them, not helping to raise, nurture, protect, provide and care for all of your children? Your ancestors were forced into this setup. What is your reason?

Those who endeavor to find a solution to the conflict among the human family, and do not research the beginning of this conflict among the family members will never arrive at nor resolve the conflict. Those who continue to believe as does the author of the old book will continue to find conflict with no resolution.

In fact those who are asked to sit on the many committees, councils or whatever will have to ask themselves "Is this a request from the Almighty God through a sinful man/woman, or is this a request from a sinful man/woman to another group of sinful men/women to continue the conflict?"

This is why it is very, very important for all to understand that people can pass as many laws as this earth can hold. In fact man has made a law for everything. You name it, there is a law for it or against it. People can legislate and pass as many laws as they want to, but they can not legislate hearts, and you can not be in the midst of the secret meetings/teaching of these who are continuing niggerism under niggerology.

African and African Americans were placed in a Godless, immoral, broken family, joblessness, noneducation, poor housing, prisons, alcohol, drugs; and a non-political participation fast track for over 400 years. The propaganda that was used to teach groups of humans how to keep the human families of Africans and African American on this fast track even down to this day was never disclosed to Africans and the African American group.

The fast track information groups used many organizations, instruments and teachings to carry out the "big lie". This research is aimed at helping all who are saying that they are working toward peaceful human (race) relations among African Americans and White Americans. The goal is to start on the "information highway" being "nigger word" literate. Those who have access to this information can help those of us from whom this information has been withheld. Nothing and no one can resolve a conflict until the person learns where, what, when, why, and who the conflict came from.

We are not saying that the research that

you have read and digested is true. But, it was taught and applied as truth about the African and African American group then and now. We believe that this is the source of the "nigger word". African Americans have made some of this teaching true because of not knowing about this teaching, and because of the many things being withheld from them such as owning land, producing for the market, having quality jobs, having quality housing, and obtaining the education that the test are designed from, and having the freedom to read, study and apply God's teachings in his/her everyday life in the 1600.

You are dealing with a conflict that is/was born from these finding and is structured on the research that you have been reading.

Human relations (race relations) will never get better until everyone removes from the vocabulary, heart, and mind the word "race". There is only one human group on this earth, and any one who believes in/uses this word, that one can not help to solve the conflict. In fact, the continuing use of the word "race" will elevate one group, and control and dominate the other group.

History will show how this happened in America. Any book that you will read pertaining to slavery (Africans - African Americans) will almost always talk about three areas which Africans and African Americans were systematically locked out of, and forced into another direction. The three areas are God, government, and family. Separating families from the beginning, denying marriage between the male and female, and forcing unwanted sexual relaitonship between the male and female to reproduce a child/children without the benefit of family, and the name of his/her father was a familiar act. The children and parents were used for the "labor plan", with children saying "I don't have a daddy". The parent was afraid to tell the child/children his/her father's name. This is also the beginning of American's so-called illegitimacy, and that spirit has passed down to 1995. America is illegitmate, not children or parents. America owes child support from 1500-1995. We say this because of the forced familiar acts mentioned above. To reinforce all of this, Africans and African Americans were not allowed to work and receive the amount of money that they were laboring for. African Americans learned of help that the Federal and State governments could give to them during the depression of the 1930's which would keep their families together also. But, women were told that they could not have a man in the house. So, here was another attack to break down many strong African American families that had survived reconstruction. After the end of the so-called "legalized segregation", African Amercians had to go out into the United States' work force and apply for a job from the children of the very people who enslaved their ancestors, them and their children. The African American males in particular were not given work; instead European white women and emigrants with or without education were hired. African Americans were denied jobs because they were "not qualified". How can a people build a country and not be qualified to work?

It is time to make a change. We only have four years before the twenty-first century to restructure and empower our minds, hearts and actions to be morally clean. Never mind man and his fix-it machines. But, we must start by studying the universe and the Creator of it so that we can come back in harmony with this Supreme Being. Each one of us must start in our own family first. There must be a code of morality taught in each home. Our children must be taught the same moral standards. It does not matter where we live, who we are or what we believe in.

Those who wrote the old book which We have presented to you under the title *Mommie, What is A Nigger, The Case of the Centuries* stated almost in each chapter that the negro is not even African. The negro is a beast, and was made (not created) a beast by God from the beginning. The beast-negro was made as the highest level of the ape family. The beast-negro was to reproduce its kind. The reproduction of its kind would be used for the benefit of doing the "laborious work" which the man (white-human) by using his mental faculties to look at God's creation and draw up plans which would extract things from the creation to be built, planted . . . . . . , and only used by the human (white).

When God kept turning down Cain's sacrifice, it was because Cain had already gone out and had sexual contact with one of the female beasts-negroes. The anger from Cain toward his brother Abel because Cain's sacrifice was not acceptable moved Cain to murder his brother. God, sent Cain into another land with his female-beast negro, according to the aforementioned researcher.

Misery is to be over come. This research is to help all of us (African Americans and European Americans) to overcome the misery of the "niggerology" institutions. We must start the healing from the cancer of superiority which has kept its position because of being grounded into the three strongest institution in America.

The "nigger word" started from some using the Bible to prove and set up the cancer of racism. Each one of us must slow down, and stop to meditate upon who really created us? What was the purpose of your being born on American soil for some, having emigrated for others, and being forced into slavery for others. Why did the Supreme Being allow this? If we seek to know the answers to these questions, isn't it only common sense to understand that the Supreme Being would have something on this earth to help us? We believe the Bible is that something, and we respect every other person who might have another teaching.

We recently read a book in which the author said "I had always gone to school with children of all backgrounds in Pennsylvania, Kansas, France, and Germany, and had never thought much about it............. In 1962 I found myself in my first political argument about race, listening to a yellow-dog Democrat from Cairo (deep in South Georgia) patiently explain how Blacks were not fully human and that any effort to integrate was biologically doomed to fail."

The mere fact that the author felt a need to include the above information in the book proves again that the researched information had and is still being taught in some form.

You take your "information highway." Give us (family) forty acres and our mule. While you are sitting down talking to your computer, we will be tilling our land to grow our food, and we will deliver you some fresh food for you to eat, to take care of your eyes, and your entire body, as radiation, confusion, immoral information, stealing and more lying come across the screen, as you sit for hours doing nothing - becoming a vegetable.

We still stand by the nine year game plan that we suggested in the book *I Cry For My Parents*. This book was written in 1990. We only have four years left before entering the twenty-first century. How will you enter? Will you enter with the heart, mind and action of the opinion expressed by the plaintiffs, or will you enter with the heart, mind, and action of the defendants refuting the opinions expressed?

Some have theorized, categorized and labeled African Americans and their children. There are volumes of books written against them. Some people are reading and applying the negatives that are stated against them. For once in your lives, African American, theorize, categorize and label yourselves. Activate your true genius. Help yourselves and your children, particularly your sons, activate what is in them.

Your ancestors came from Africa, and you were created by the Almighty God. You are an innate-genius, innately intelligent, with innate ability (IGIA). Your IGIA is deeply rooted in Matthew 25: 14-30. The IGIA spirit is that which was created in us--born into us. It is not arrived at through experience(s). The IGIA spirit is good, shareable, creative, inventive, productive, sensible, storable, retrievable, understanding and will adjust to new situations. Therefore, the IGIA person will always seek to be a part of the creative, inventive, productive forces. He or she having this spirit can never be oppressed totally. They are always striving for and working toward human rights.

There is still time to activate and start developing your genius before you enter the twenty-first century; therefore you should carry with you into the 21st century the spirit that your forefathers brought with them from Africa in the 16th century. That spirit was of creativity, invention and production. The IGIA came from our forefathers even though they were subjected to the worst brutality that has ever been done to any group of people, but there are historical documents that will prove that the African-American man was and is a genius.

The criminal activity that you are seeing today by some of your children (mainly our sons) caused Charles Silbermans in his book *Criminal Violence, Criminal Justice* to suggest that African Americans are hosts to a dreadful disease, a kind of innate violence. This activity is none other than the suppressed IGIA crying out to be recognized, activated, and used.

African-American male, children are labeled as aggressive, a leader, (bad leader) talkative, (not knowing when to shut up), destructive, and having the spirit of a criminal. So some are saying that maybe these children are thinking and, in some cases, saying "What have I got to lose?"

If many of your sons are asking themselves why they are becoming human commodity (prisoners), then maybe we can shed some light upon their premeditated loss. We say to them: You have yourself to lose. You can lose the chance of not ever knowing what you really could have achieved creatively. You can lose the chance of becoming a working class citizen - the difference between freedom and prison. You have the IGIA abilities in you to lose.

You must ask yourselves an honest question. What do I want to work at during and after I have graduated (diploma, not a GED) from my schooling? Once you have honestly done this, then you will have to keep this before you at all times. You must become a good reader. Read about everything and everyone who has become successful in his field. If it is an idea that has not been seen or heard about yet, write it down and keep it to yourself. Time will come when you will develop your idea further, bring it into being, securing your idea.

The mere fact that certain groups of people have been suppressed from using their IGIA, this can cause these people to rebel. So the labeling definitions that have been applied to you, my sons, are not true ones. It was, and it is, their IGIA creative ability that is crying out to be used. Do not rebel in the form that will result in your becoming human commodity (prisoner). Rebel in the fact of now enhancing that ability to its utmost. Go to school and close your mouth in the classes. Learn something for that day. Spend quality time doing all of your homework every day. Make good grades and watch how your

IGIA will activate and grow. The years of education are going to roll around real fast. Become active in all sports. You love cars! Learn how to make your own and fix them now while you are being educated. You love having money to spend. Educate yourself in the field that you are interested in, and develop a business of your own, therefore generating a job, money and a job for someone else. You can do it. Your activated IGIA is in you to help you to become whatever you want to become.

"What have you got to lose." You have your mother's love, your father's love and the Almighty God's love and power to lose. Your parents did not birth you on this earth to become a death or prison statistic, and certainly not before you can get out of the sixth grade. Listen to your parents. They have a plan that will save you from prison or death.

So, parents, what can you do? There are some people even in the school system that are capitalizing upon the fact that some of our children do not have the protection and guidance from both parents. Parents, you are responsible for and to your children. African American fathers if you are not married to or are separated from girlfriends or wives, you must take an active role in your child's education and behavior in the classroom, school, and outside in the community. You discipline your child and help to educate and raise him/her. This statement is not suggesting that you become intimate with the parent again, and parents do not misunderstand this as rekindling a relationship. It means exactly what is said. All parents make an effort to take an active, loving, protective, providing, teaching, caring and supportive role in your child or children lives. So, for some parents it will mean that your family will include all of your children whether you are married or single. Make room for saving your children, because of what you learned from the "old book". Help them to know who they are (Leviticus 18:). Raise your sons/daughters to become good, moral daters, husband/wife, father/mother, thus returning the African American family to the Almighty God.

African American fathers, your name, address, and telephone numbers (job and home) should be on the school records. Even if you live in another state, country or etc., you should know at all times what is happening with your blood. No one should stand in the way if you really want to do this. We do know that many of you are in favor of what we stated above. We met and talked to you. You must do this now for yourself and your children.

There is a child support law that says that you will go to jail if you do not help to support yours. Many times mothers know that you cannot meet these payments, and you are taken off your job and placed in jail. What if that law would have read, if you cannot make payments, you must spend "community time" with your child. "Community time" would incorporate all the things that are mentioned in the above paragraphs. Children need to be nurtured by both parents.

Instead, the law said "We cannot force you to spend time with your child." But at the same time, the law can "force you into jail."

You can bring the spirit of your children out of the prison wall. How? By praying honestly together about such. Take your children into a prison. Let them see what it is all about ("Prison is a very lonely place"). We took our son when he was three years old.

Become an active member of your PTO or PTA association. If there are 600 students in the school, there should be 600 parents attending PTA meetings. PTA/PTO executive board members must be aware of the actitives that they vote to have parents and their children participant in. Parents and their children have become excellent sales persons. It is okay to sell candy as a school wide activity, but it is not okay to conduct a school wide activity for parents to build self-esteem, raise the conscience level toward empowering and restructing the minds, hearts and actions of all the parents toward a positive goal as a group? When it comes to the parent activity those in charge almost always ask "is it free?"

Nothing is free. You will pay one way or another. There are many programs that have been structured by African Americans. These programs can/will empower the family and restructure the mind, heart and action of the family for good. But sadly to say that there are those who are still asking "is it free?" "It is an excellent program but the parents can not afford it," or something to this effect?

Make your school function as a private school for you and your child. How? Discuss a dress code for your school from kindergarten up to the twelfth grade. (This is an idea that must be discussed with other parents). How can a dress code benefit you, your child, teachers, and most of all, activate IGIA?

African Americans are the lowest paid of all, but they spend more money than any other group of people on clothing, and they have more children in school at the same time. Enforcing a dress code will alleviate a great deal of financial burdens from your pocketbook. Your child will go into the classroom with others that will have on the same colors, at least, as he or she does. This will remove the constant concentration on fashion, therefore freeing the teacher to go on with the teaching of the subject for that day, forcing your child to become an active participant in his education. You will be saving money that will help your family through the financial hardships that we all experience at one time or another. You need a vacation; your children need to be exposed to other areas of his world.

The saving of such money can do many things for you and your family.

Most African American do not have enough money to put their children into private school, but they must be intelligent enough to recognize the power that they have as parents. No, not everyone will understand this plan and go along with it. But it is a plan that must be dealt with if they want to save their children and themselves some heartfelt tears. African American children belong to them. The parents are the ones who have gone through the birth pains, no one else. It seems that some believe that African Americans do not have any authority over what is to happen to their children. Some believe that African Americans are just having babies to have them. Well, only you know the real reason, but since God has allowed them to be born, let's be caretakers of his blessing. Turn off the T.V. from Monday-Friday. **You must control your household. To the point parents - get involved with your child!**

Some teachers are teaching and they are keeping themselves abreast with all of the new curriculum that seem to change every five years.

Therefore, they learn a new teaching method each time a good one began to work and someone wants to experiment with his/her new idea. But some are saying that the educational system in the United States is not producing a positive work ethic in citizens.

Well, just as the children (at least the African American children) need to know what is in them and strive for that, and parents need to know how to structure their power in order to gain back their children from prison and death (at least African American parents), then some principals and some teachers must also have a hand in all areas of education.

One of the greatest areas that needs improvement is the number of children in a classroom from 1 through 12 grades. This is a given: Children are dealing with more than they ever had to in the history of the World. If we were to even start elaborating upon such it would turn out to be volumes of books. So we will get to our point. No one teacher should have a class size of more than 15-20 students. The maximum should be twenty. Teachers are about loving and educating bright minds, watching that face light up. Teachers with the art of teaching are about generating citizens.

We need more educational assistants. Parents, here is another area in which you can help. There are some parents who would not let it rest if they found that their child was in an oversized class. Yes, even one parent can make a difference.

Leave the negative labels to those who found them, and try to teach others against some in the human family. You know who you are, where you came from, and what is in you.

Do not cry anymore or be labeled with "African American on African American crime". You have four years left in this century. You must be about the business of activating your IGIA now so that you will not bring the niggerism spirit into the twenty-first century. But instead you must carry the spirit of creativeness, productiveness, the spirit of Matthew 25:14-30.

We love you my African and African American families. Thank God that we were born into the African-American group of the human family. The Supreme Being could have deemed that we should not have been born at all.

Africans were born for a positive purpose on this earth.

On the day that my maternal grandmother died, she said to her ten children, "You all be good to each other."

You all be good to each other, parents to children and children to parents. On the day of my maternal grandfather's first marriage, Thomas "Jeffie" Jackson, he wrote that he was married in the presence of "some white friends". So this is a closing to all of his "white friends" which we have accepted as our "white friends" also. Let's be good to each other.

Let the healing begin. Never leave God. African American Ancestors kept their hands, hearts and minds in/on God. Pray all the time. Never give up this most intimate line of communication between you and the Almighty God. Spend quality time reading, meditating and the acting. Marriage is God's arrangement. If you have children, teach them about God, work, family and the government. We leave with you the following educational assignments. Read each one of these books immediately in a family group:

1. *Bible*
2. *Mommie, What is a Nigger?*
3. *AlphaBlack Culture Beginning Activity Book*
4. *I Cry For My Parents*
5. *The Mis-Education of the Negro*

What is a Nigger? You have learned what the plaintiffs' assumed theory is. Why are some Caucasian using the word now? The old book has revealed that there was/is a teaching among some of the Caucasian group using this theory as truth.

The Almighty God in His mystery will always know the real truth. You can not lie on the Almighty God, and make Him back up your lie. He is the Juror and Judge of our lives. (Romans 3:4, Revelation 1:8-16).

So, I just want to hear the grass grow, see the wind blow, and smell the sun as it goes down.

SUGGESTED READINGS

1. Bible Exodus 22:22-24, 29: Malachi 4:6; Jeremiah 5:28.

2. Isaac, Mia. *I Cry For My Parents*. IGIA Publisher & Distributing, Columbia, South Carolina, 1990.

3. Isaac, Mia. *AlphaBlack Culture Beginning Activity*. IGIA Publisher & Distributing, Columbia, South Carolina, 1991.

4. Author Unknown.

5. All books that are written by African American authors.

6. Kaplan, Sidney. *The Black Presence in the Era of the American Revolution* 1770-1800. Connecticut: New York Graphic Society, 1973 pages 110-241. Read carefully pages 220-223, 216-217, 214-215, 212-213, 209-211, 150-170, 147-149, 111-128.

7. Forner, Philip S. *History of Black Americans*. Connecticut: Greenwood Press, 1975 pages 120-123, 292-306, 283-288, 166-167, 537-551.

SUGGESTED READINGS

8. Poski, Harry, Marr, II, Warren. *The Negro Almanac*. New York: The Bellwether Company, 1976.

9. Wesley, Charles H. *Afro-American Life and History*. Pennsylvania: The Publishers Agency, Inc. Volume 1 through 6.

10. Dubois, W. E. B. *Black Folk, Then and Now: An Essay in the History and Sociology of the Negro Race*. New York, 1939.

11. Bennett, Lerone, Jr. *Before the Mayflower: A History of the Negro in America*, 1619-1964. Chicago, 1964.

12. Garnet, Henry Highland. *The Past and the Present Condition, and the Destiny, of the Colored Race*. Troy, N.Y., 1884.

13. XXVII (October 1942). _____. *The Negro in the Making of America*. New York, 1964.

14. Sloan, Irving J. *The American Negro: A Chronology and Fact Book*. Dobbs Ferry, N.Y., 1965.

15. Thrope, Earle E. *The Mind of the Negro:*

SUGGESTED READINGS

An Interllectual History of Afro-Americans. Baton Rouge, 1961.

16. Washington, Booker T. *The Story of the Negro: The Rise of the Race from Slavery.* Garden City, N. Y., 1909.

17. Washington, Booker T. *An Autobiography: The Story of My Life and Work.* J. L. Nichols & Company. Naperville, Illinois, 1901.

18. U.S. Bureau of the Census. *Negro Population in the United States:* 1790-1915. Washington, 1918.

19. Van Deusen, John G. *The Black Man in White America.* Washington, 1938.

20. Allen, Richard, and Jones, Absalom. *A Narrative of the Proceedings of the Black People during the Late Awful Calamity in Philadelphia, in the Year 1793.* Philadelphia, 1794.

21. Forner, Philip S. *History of Black Americans. From Africa to the Emergence of the cotton kingdom.* Connecticut, Greenwood Press, 1975, Vol. 1

SUGGESTED READINGS

22. Forner, Philip S. *History of Black Americans. Eve of the compromise* of 1850. Connecticut, Greenwood Press, 1983, Vol. 2

23. Forner, Philip S. *History of Black Americans. To he end of the Civil War.* Connecticut, Greenwood Press, 1983, Vol. 3

24. Chase, Allan. *The Legacy of Malthus. The Social costs of the new scientific racism.* New York. Alfred A. Knopf, Inc. 1975

25. Aptheker, Herbert. *History of the Negro People in the United States.* New York, Caro Publishing. Vol. 1, 2, 3, 4, 5, 6

26. Newby, I. A. *Black Carolinians. A History of Blacks in South Carolina from 1895 to 1968.* Columbia, University of South Carolina Press, 1973.

27. Barnwell, William H. *In Richard's World. The Battle of Charleston 1966.* Boston, Houghton Mifflin Company, 1968

28. Weltner, Charles Longstreet. *Southerner.* New York, J. B. Lippincott Company, 1966

29. Miller, John Chester. *The Wolf By The*

SUGGESTED READINGS

Ears. Thomas Jefferson and Slavery. New York, Collier MacMillan Publishers, 1977 page 124 - , 164

30. Dollard, John. *Caste and Class in Southern Town*. New York, Doubleday Anchor Books, 1937. pages 352 ___

31. Webber, Thomas, L. *Deep Like the Rivers*. New York, W. W. Norton & Company, 1978.

32. Washington, B. T. *The American Negro*. New York, Arno Press, 1969. pg. 74

33. Madhubutl, Hakl R. *Black Men, The Afrikan American Family in Transition*. Chicago, Third World Press, 1990 page 94 - page 127

34. Berlin, Ira. *Slaves Without Masters*. New York. Pantheon Books, 1974

35. Carroll, Joseph Cephas. *Slave Insurrections In The United States* 1800-1865. New York, Negro Universities Press {David Walker pg 122}

36. Escott, Paul D. *Slavery Remembered*. North Carolina. The University of North Carolina Press, 1979.

SUGGESTED READINGS

37. Mullin, Michael. *American Negro Slavery.* Columbia, University of South Carolina Press, 1976.

38. Adoff, Arnold. *Black on Black: Commentaries by Negro American.* New York, MacMillan Company, 1968 page 23 & 24.

39. Brown, William Wells. *My Southern Home.* New York, Negro Universities Press. 1880 {regard slaves as cattle, preached that slaves should do what the master said.

40. Rawick, George P. *The American Slave: A Composite Autobiography.* Connecticut, Greenwood Publishing Company, 1941 pages 62, 63 {a former slave talks about the house the family lived in, food eaten, working and no education.} pages 66, 67 Samuel Boilware uses the "nigger word" also said "African eat people" page 127-130

41. Tindall, George Brown. *South Carolina Negroes 1877-1900.* Columbia. University of South Carolina, 1952 (This book has pictures of "Negroes in Politic - Robert B. Anderson, I. R. Reed, Robert Smalls, William J. Whipper, James Wigg & Thomas E. Miller were the negro members of the constitutional convention of SC 1895: pages 294).

SUGGESTED READINGS

42. Koger, Larry. *Black Slave Owners. Free Black Slave Masters in South Carolina.* 1790-1860. North Carolina, McFarland & Company, Inc., Publisher 1958.

43. Federal Writers' Project. *Slave Narratives.* Michigan, Scholarly Press, Inc. 1976.

44. The Southern Society for the Promotion of the Study of Race Conditions and Problems in the South. Race problems of the south. New York, Negro Universities Press, 1900 page 92 (AA Teachers)

45. Sutherland, Robert L. *Color, Class and Personality.* Connecticut, Greenwood Press, Publisher. 1942.

46. Sterling, Dorothy. *The Trouble they Seen. Black people tell the story of Reconstruction.* New York, Doubleday & Company, 1976.

47. Reese, Mildred L. *America and U.S.* Philadelphia, Dorrance & Company, 1975.

48. Pickens, Williams. *The New Negro.* New York, Negro Universities Press, 1916. (pages 34, 35)

49. Perkins, Eugene. *Home is a Dirty Street.*

SUGGESTED READINGS

Chicago, Third World Press, 1975.

    50. Nielson, David Gordon. *Black Ethos.* Connecticut, Greenwood Press, 1977 (re-read pages 50)

    51. Gist, Noel P. *The Blending of Races.* New York, Wiley - Interscience, 1972 (page 3).

    52. Smith, Carter. *American Historical Images on File, The Black Experience.* New York, Facts on File. 1990. pgs. 3.10, 3.11 & 3.12, 3.1, 3.15, 3.20, *3.22, *3.25

    53. Schlesinger, Jr. Arthur M. *History of American. Presidential Elections.* New York, Chelsea House Publishers, 1971. Volume 1, 2.

    54. Kavenagh, W. Keith. *Foundations of Colonial America.* New York, Chelsea House Publisher, 1973.

    55. Snodgrass, Mary Ellen. *Black History Month - Resource Book.* Detroit, Gale Research Inc. 1993.

    56. Brewer, J. Mason. *American Negro Folklore.* Chicago Quadrangle Book, 1968.

SUGGESTED READINGS

57. Gutman, Herbert G. *Who Built America?* New York, Patheon Books, 1989. Vol 1 and Vol. 2

GLOSSARY

INNATE

1. existing in one from birth - inborn.

2. Was and is existing in a person at birth.

3. concepts present in the mind at birth as opposed to concepts arrived at through experience.

4. existing in a person from birth, inborn "as a essential characteristic."

5. Native to, or original with the individual, inborn, natural.

6. to be born in, originate in, existing naturally rather than acquired.

GENIUS

1. guardian spirit, natural ability according to Roman belief, a guardian spirit assigned to a person at birth; a guardian spirit of any person supposed to influence one's destiny. A great natural ability - strong disposition or inclination, great mental capacity and inventive ability, creative.

2. exceptional intellectual and creative power. One who possess exceptional and creative power, natural.

3. **Pagan**: attendant spirit allotted to everyone at his birth, to govern his fortunes and determine his character.

Christian: The two mutually opposed spirits by whom every person was suppose to be attended throughout his life. Hence, applied to a person who powerfully influences for good or evil the character, conduct, or fortunes of another.

Roman: guardian spirit of a man, a family, or a state. As a guardian spirit of an individual. Notable achievements or high intellectual powers of an individual were attributed to his genius, and ultimately a man of achievements was said to have genius or to be a genius.

INTELLIGENCE
1. having or showing an alert mind; bright, perceptive, clever, wise.

2. to see into, perceive, understand, sensible

3. in psychology, the general mental ability involved in calculating, reasoning, perceiving relationships, and analogies, learning quickly, storing and retrieving information.... adjusting to new situation.

4. having good understanding or high mental capacity, quick.

NIGGERISM - doctrine or theory that assume that the negro (African and African American) is sub-human

NIGGEROLOGY - The study of niggerism

DICTIONARIES

1. The Random House Dictionary

2. The American Heritage Dictionary

3. The Oxford English Dictionary

4. Funk and Wagnalls Standard Comprehensive International Dictionary

5. Webster's New World Dictionary

6. The New Columbia Encyclopedia

Mia Isaac was born in Columbia, South Carolina and reared in North, South Carolina and Brooklyn, New York. A teacher for 23 years. Ten year in Brooklyn, New York, 13 years in Columbia, South Carolina and other states. Mia Isaac was educated at Long Island University in Brooklyn and Long Island University Graduate School, Fordham University, New York, Bishop College, Dallas, Texas, University of South Carolina and Columbia College, Columbia, South Carolina.

Mia Isaac has authored *I Cry For My Parents and AlphaBlack Culture Beginning Activity Books*, and founded the IGIA Leadership/Academy Programs for parents and children. She has appeared on television and radio programs within the United States, and travels to different states speaking to fathers, mothers and children about activating their IGIA now and into the 21st Century.

Received an incentive award from Richland District #1 in the school year 1988/89. Received an award from parents in the school year of 1983/84 in Brooklyn, New York. Received an award from South Carolina State University for the BCDI - 1993.

www.ingramcontent.com/pod-product-compliance
Lightning Source LLC
Chambersburg PA
CBHW060110170426
43198CB00010B/842